M

Have You Seen My Leather Pants?

Onyxx, publicity photo, 1990.

Mom, Have You Seen My Leather Pants?

THE TALE OF A TEEN ROCK WANNABE WHO ALMOST WAS

CRAIG A. WILLIAMS

Three Rivers Press / New York

Published in the United States by Three Rivers Press, an imprint of the
Crown Publishing Group, a division of Random House, Inc., New York.
www.crownpublishing.com

Three Rivers Press and the Tugboat design are registered trademarks of
Random House, Inc.

Library of Congress Cataloging-in-Publication Data

Williams, Craig A.
    Mom, have you seen my leather pants? : the tale of a teen rock
wannabe who almost was / Craig A. Williams—1st ed.
      1. Williams, Craig A.   2. Rock musicians—United States—
Biography. 3. Onyxxx (Musical group)   I. Title.
    ML420. W543A3 2007
    782.42166092—dc22
    [B]
                                                        2007014954
    ISBN 978-0-307-34212-6

Printed in the United States of America

Design by Elina D. Nudelman

10 9 8 7 6 5 4 3 2 1

First Edition

To Mom and Dad

Acknowledgments

I was going to write these acknowledgments in the style of the inside sleeve of a Crüe album, but I didn't want to belittle any of the following people by claiming that this book was written on "Foster's Lager, Budweiser, Bombay Gin, lots of Jack Daniels, Kahlúa and Brandy, Quackers and Krell, and Wild Women!" Besides, anyone who knows me would know it to be a front. I rarely drink lager.

I'll thank my parents first, to whom this book is dedicated, not because I think they'll like it, but because they've always allowed me to be as I am.

"Thank you" is hardly enough for Melissa, who was always available, regardless of what she was doing, to come into my office and provide insight. I can't tell you how much I think of you during my guitar solos. I hope your family will still talk to me.

Joe Piscatella I have to thank not only for his notes, but for his patience and friendship. Your dedication to *Guitar Hero* is an inspiration.

A heartfelt thanks to Patrick Sauer, whose theory on Van Halen is simply superb.

Un milion de gracias to Scott Johnson, who sent me notes all the way from San Salvador. Send me some *papusas,* too.

I have to thank the man known in these pages as "Sonny." He was always available for some ridiculous question or another, even while seeing a patient.

Craig: What was your reaction when I learned how to play "Eruption"?

Sonny: I said, "If you can play that, we're totally going to get signed."

Craig: That's what I thought. Hilarious.

Sonny: Hey, remember when you said, "Jimi Hendrix invented the rock guitar, and Eddie Van Halen saved it"?

Craig: Dude, I was sixteen. Lay off.

Sonny: You're the one writing the book.

Patient: Doctor, I can't feel the left side of my body.

Sonny: I gotta go.

We can all be grateful to "Kul" and the entire "Gupta" clan for holding on to an Onyxx demo all these years.

My thanks to Robert Lazar at ICM, who saw something in these first few chapters, and got them over to Richard Abate, who also deserves my gratitude.

Carrie Thornton, my editor, thank you for liking my book enough to help make it better.

I have to thank Judith Grossman, Geoffrey Wolff, and Hubert Selby Jr., who cavorted with rock stars aplenty.

Heather Miles deserves a thank you for being one of the first people to read the opening chapters and encouraging me to keep going on it.

Thanks to William Brown, who was actually at the Long Beach Arena during the recording of Iron Maiden's *Live After Death.* You keep the rock alive.

Thanks to Tim and Amita, for our country jams and taco Tuesdays—if we start a new band, Tim, you can totally be in it.

Acknowledgments

Thank you to the doctor's and nurses of Century City Doctor's Hospital.

Finally, I have to acknowledge John Jacobs, Jeff Frankel, Jacob Kornbluth, my big sister, Jen, all my friends and family, and my neighbors, who were forced by proximity to listen to my "Leather Pants Mix," often at inconvenient hours.

Become my friend, hear some authentic Onyxx tunes, and tell me about your rock star fantasy at myspace.com/myleatherpants.

Contents

Contents

Author's Note

Due to the rather lurid, morally questionable, and outright illegal nature of some of the activities depicted in the following pages, I have taken it upon myself to change the names of virtually everyone involved with this story to protect their privacy.

I should also point out, since people discover a bizarre brand of outrage when there appears to be some imprecision in their nonfiction, that conversations and events in this book have been recounted to the best of my memory.

Caution: This book contains backward messages!

Mutha
(Don't Want to
Go to
School Today)

When I was sixteen years old, I autographed breasts.

This was not a fluke. Nor was it my prize in a bet with the town hoochie. This was just something I did when I was that age. Sign things. Scraps of paper. Notebooks. Ticket stubs. And once, breasts. Because between the ages of fourteen and seventeen, I was a rock star.

It is a condition from which you never truly recover. Once you've admitted the problem to yourself, however, you're on the road to recovery. I am still very much on this road. Even now, rare is the day when I don't fantasize about being on stage again, crammed hot and sweaty into some dark hole with the sweet smell of hairspray, spritz spray, and scrunch spray in the air. It is only now, many years after the fact, that I can speak honestly and openly about my life as a rock star.

I don't use the term lightly, and I am fully aware that it has been poached to near meaninglessness. "How was Vegas?" one might ask a friend. To which said friend might reply, "Dude, we partied like rock stars." The phrase has entered the lexicon of college students, twenty-somethings, and even the marketers of energy drinks, and as a recovering rock star, I take offense. Certainly, if the response were "I drank so much I was retarded," the reaction from the Disabled Persons of America would be one of outrage. Rock stars, as of yet, have no political lobby and therefore must endure such bigotry.

Going to a strip club does not make one a rock star. Going to your senior prom with a stripper, as our singer did, does. Drinking gobs and gobs of whiskey does not make one a rock star. Headlining a sold-out gig at the Whisky A Go-Go on the Sunset Strip, as my band did, does. Having multiple sexual partners does not make one a rock star. Having groupies does.

I had groupies—girls my age to women ten years my senior. They put me up in hotels, bought me booze, and let me borrow their cars. They taught me things.

I wore leather pants and suede cowboy boots—to high school—had hair down to my ass, knew grown men with names like Trashy and Freak, sold out weekend nights at Hollywood's storied venues, such as the Roxy, Gazzarri's, and The Troubadour. I wrote songs that made dozens of people sing.

At some point, however, this existence contrasted with my other reality—that of an honors student at Canyon High School in Orange County, California. My home was in the burg of Yorba Linda, where, it should be noted, more than 2 percent of all U.S. presidents were born. It is a place of endless tract housing, red-tiled roofs creeping onto rolling hills, bordered by the Riverside Freeway tracing the bottom of the canyon, a congested thoroughfare that leads to Los Angeles, a drive of an hour or so to the northwest.

My parents were not necessarily pleased by my rock star ambition. My mom, who had encouraged me to explore music from the time I was seven, called it a pipe dream. The only time my dad raised his hand against me was when my band started gigging in Hollywood on school nights. Then there were the awkward moments when I started getting calls from women with names like "Baby."

"Um, honey," my mom said, as she came out from the kitchen to the family room one evening. "Phone's for you."

I was sprawled across the sofa watching MTV. "Who is it?"

"She said her name's Baby?" Note that the answer was phrased as a question in an effort to gather information without sounding nosy. A classic maternal trick.

Had I fallen for it, I would have told her that Baby used to be a stripper at The Cave on Hollywood Boulevard but had quit to focus on phone sex full time. And that some nights, rather than doing my geometry homework, I would help Baby with her routine.

"I'll take it upstairs." I flipped off the TV, casually sprinted to my room, and shut the door.

As a result, my grades suffered. Listening to Baby's midnight lectures was far more engaging than listening to Mr. Smoke drone on about the importance of geometry. I failed geometry. I had other things on my mind. Like how Baby might sound softly enunciating the word *hypotenuse*.

Or autographing breasts.

People never forget their first time, and the age of sixteen held many first times for me. Yet the first time I autographed breasts seems to hold special significance. Because it is not something I do anymore. Because I don't recall there being a second time. And because most people don't have a first time.

We were called Onyx at first. Later, because an up-and-coming hip-hop group had already laid claim to that name and we received cease and desist papers from their attorney, we became Onyxx. Then Onyxxx. Then we broke up.

But that's simplifying things.

In a 1991 interview that appeared in the *Los Angeles Times*, our manager claims we were called Onyx because "*Onyx* is a multifaceted stone and as you can see, these guys are each multifaceted."

What she was so insightfully pointing out is that we were a somewhat diverse cross-section of the American melting pot. Our drummer, Kyle Siegel, was Jewish. Our bassist, Sunil "Sonny" Gupta, was Indian, at times a Hindu. Tyler Jacobs, the singer, and I, the guitarist, were vague forms of WASPs. So you can sort of see her point about being multifaceted, right?

The truth is that I found the name in a science textbook during my freshman year in high school and I liked the brevity and use of both Y and X. Other bands working The Strip at that time included Tryx and Lix, so Onyx seemed spot on.

At the time of the breast-signing incident, Onyx was booked at an all-ages club called Rock Around the Clock. This gig was a big one for us, as we were supporting Hollywood Hair Metal heavies Swingin' Thing. At that time, there was no bigger band on The Strip than Swingin' Thing. They were poised to be the next Poison. Their crowd favorite, "Let's Do It with the Lights On," warranted their being hailed as the second coming of Warrant. We knew opening for Swingin' Thing was an opportunity that would either take us to the level of elite Hollywood bands or send us back to Orange County with our Spandex between our legs.

Swingin' Thing had seen our ad that appeared regularly in *Screamer*, the free weekly that was found around the Strip. The ad contained a photo of the four of us with the band name in block letters that looked to be carved from stone. Beneath the photo was a list of upcoming show dates and in the upper right corner was the selling phrase "They're only 16!"

Apparently, it was enough to persuade Swingin' Thing's singer to approach our aforementioned manager, Barbara Tice, a genuine Loni Anderson impersonator. Barbara insisted on going by the moniker "Barbi," and her resemblance to Loni Anderson wasn't just cursory—it was actually quite unsettling. Spending time with Barbi was like hanging out with a podiatrist. That someone would dedicate so much of her life to such a specialized cause seemed inane to me, even as a rump-rocking teen. Yet her appearance at times helped garner a few fringe benefits from club owners and promoters—benefits such as limos and hotel rooms. One owner, his arm draped around Barbi in the corner of a darkened vinyl booth at his club, told us, "I get you guys all blow jobs," in some foreign accent. Only Tyler and Kyle got the blow jobs, but the decision to play this guy's club was unanimous.

Barbi also landed us this life-altering gig with Swingin' Thing. By the time we took the stage at a little after 9:00 P.M., Rock Around the Clock was filled to capacity with several hundred girls wearing tight black clothing and too much makeup and displaying hairstyles that could not safely come within fifteen feet of an open flame.

We ripped into our opening number, "Rise High," a song in which we used as many clichés in three minutes as possible to inspire people to do and be their best. Exhibit A: the chorus.

> Rise high
> Shoot for the stars
> You're only as young as you feel
> So rise high.

Needless to say, our girls were pumped, swaying their hips in the uncomfortable manner employed by white people. And we never let up throughout our forty-five minute set, from ass-kickers like "Life Behind the Scenes" to our acoustic ballad "In Your Heart" to our final and most popular song, "Another Tear."

As the stage went black, the room exploded in a cacophony of praise. Backstage, we pretended to be done, giving one another high fives, adjusting our cowboy boots, and holding our instruments in anticipation of the encore.

After about two minutes of listening to our fans whistle and chant (you didn't want to make them wait too long), we returned triumphantly and busted into an amped-up version of the Bill Haley classic "Rock Around the Clock."

The crowd loved it, despite the fact that Tyler didn't seem to know the lyrics very well, a problem that, as time went on, would prove to be chronic. When the song ended and our roadies tended to our equipment, Kyle and Tyler headed for the front of the club while Sonny and I headed for the bar in back for a "drink." (Drinking absurd quantities of booze was standard practice for our shows, but in public we pretended to be somewhat straight-laced. It was when we got back to the hotel room we rented for each gig that we would debauch ourselves and whomever came with us with booze, sexual deviancy, and, later, drugs.)

Sonny and I were swarmed by adoring fans. These were girls who, to generalize a bit, weren't necessarily in the mainstream of their high schools. But it was one fan in particular, a curly blonde with green eyes, the kind of girl who would inspire Nabokov to write, who handed me the marker. At that point, we hadn't signed many autographs, but we had signed enough to know that in addition to a pen, we were usually given something upon which to scribble our names.

Not in this case.

Instead, she smiled plainly, bit her bottom lip, and opened her suede vest. Underneath was a black lace bra, which she politely pulled out of the way, exposing what I think was a very surprised breast, as the nipple seemed to squint, annoyed by the light.

I don't know how long I stared. I'd like to think I was extremely cool about it, as if this were something I did regularly, like blow-drying my long hair straight. I smiled at Sonny, took the pen in one hand, cupped her bare breast in the other, and watched as my name magically flowed across her pale flesh.

At that moment, the music and the murmuring of the club disappeared. All I could hear and feel was her breath in my ear. The whole world, in fact, seemed to consist only of her respiration as I was captured helplessly, drawn in to her chest, spinning in an unconscious darkness alone, until by some action beyond my control I was released, reabsorbed by the rotation of the earth; the smell of sweat, alcohol, and soda; and the sound of an otherworldly voice booming over the PA.

"Ladies and gentlemen, please welcome to the stage . . . Swingin' Thing!"

Little Dreamer

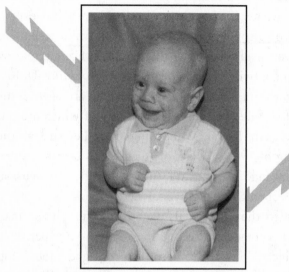

Me, at eighteen months old, fantasizing of long, luscious hair.

Rock superstardom begins as a fantasy.

The human mind is such that we all believe we are greatness waiting to be realized. For most of us, rock stardom is just a passing daydream while in the car, alone, with our favorite song on the radio. Once the song is over, or we arrive at our destination, we are the realtor, computer technician, or coffee shop attendant others see us as . . . with a secret ambition.

In our fantasies as wannabe rock stars, we are able to do things other people cannot. Play guitar like Eddie Van

Halen. Bang out the drum intro from "Hot For Teacher." Do one of those karate kicks like David Lee Roth in the "Jump" video. This is escapism. This is catharsis. This is healthy. This keeps the horrible quotidian state of our existences from suffocating us.

When we get too caught up in the fantasy, however, it mutates into something pathological. In mild cases, this disease can lead to poor fashion choices, bizarre mating habits, and a twisted sense of the word *grooming*. Unfortunately, the majority of rock star cases are severe, the result of self-destructive mindsets, two of which are put forth by Hair Metal philosophers Def Leppard at the beginning of 1983's "Rock of Ages": "It's better to burn out, than fade away" and the seemingly nonsensical "Unta gleeben glauten gloven."

While to the average listener the latter phrase may appear encrypted, to a recovering rock star, it is perfectly intelligible. "Don't try to become a rock god," Joe Elliot, lead singer of the Def, seems to have been saying in his made-up hobbit language, "or you might sever an arm in a car accident, as our drummer is going to do about a year from now, or drink yourself to death, as our guitarist is going to do in 1991." Because what Mr. Elliot knows, as do all rock stars in convalescence, is that once the disease takes hold, it rarely ends well.

Researchers agree that the transformation of this healthy fantasy to unwholesome lifestyle is idiopathic. Certainly, a mixture of karaoke and alcohol may trigger brief fits, as can awards shows (it's fun to imagine whom we might thank) and showers (something to do with acoustics; as any rock star can tell you, reverb is everything). Yet for long-term sufferers, the causes are much more mysterious, making prevention nearly impossible.

Those who are concerned that a loved one may be infected might look for the following symptoms:

- **Adding unnecessary syllables to monosyllabic words**
  While this is common practice throughout the rock star world, there is no better case study on this matter than W. Axl Rose. Compare Bob Dylan's version of "Knockin' on Heaven's Door" to that of Guns N' Roses, in which Axl saddles the word *door* with surplus syllables. The word *mine*, as in "Sweet Child O'" contains anywhere from two to five syllables. And then there is the megasyllabic ending to "Don't Cry," which lasts a sickly twenty-five seconds. Axl is almost certainly the greatest rock star to come out of the Hair Metal era, and yet today he only occasionally leaves his home to rerecord the same album he's been working on for a dozen years and beat up fashion designers. Had his illness been detected early, he might still be a productive member of society.

- **The urge to dress like a cowboy, despite the fact that you don't ride a horse or work with cattle** Clearly, no one suffers this symptom more than Jon Bon Jovi, as evidenced by "Wanted: Dead or Alive," a song in which he describes riding steel horses and carrying loaded six strings. People are quick to forget JBJ's solo career, however, during which he made a whole cowboy album (*Blaze of Glory*) for the 1994 cowboy movie *Young Guns II*. He even brought his Jersey cowboy image to his acting debut in that film as "Pit Inmate Shot Back Into Pit." I saw the movie in a theater just to witness his imaginary demise, really a symbolic moment for the entire Hair Metal community. Yet Mr. Bon Jovi hardly stands alone on this matter, as cowboy boots, chaps, and fringed suede jackets are endemic to the wannabe rocker population.

- **Changing your birth name to something that sounds like an auto part, a verb, or something European** Just look at Guns N' Roses: William Bailey became Axl Rose. Saul Hudson became Slash. Andrew Michael McKagan became Duff. Jeffrey Dean Isbell became Izzy Stradlin. Even our favorite cowboy Jon Bon Jovi was actually born John Francis Bongiovi Jr. W.A.S.P. had Blackie Lawless, the Crüe had Nikki Sixx, Faster Pussycat had Taime Downe (pronounced "Tie Me Down"), Hanoi Rocks had Razzle, and so on. I knew I had lost a friend forever when this young man officially changed his name from Mike to *Michel* and dressed up his last name by changing a few letters around and giving himself an *accent aigu*. He disappeared in the rock star ether and, to my knowledge, has yet to reappear.

Despite early detection, by the time symptoms appear, it's often too late. Should you or a loved one show signs of infection, the best you can hope for is that no permanent damage is caused.

For me, the first signs of disease appeared when I was seven, in the waning months of the Jimmy Carter administration. I'd lie awake most nights, rapt not with dreams of playing big-league ball or fighting fires, but of playing guitar for Olivia Newton John while listening to the *Xanadu* soundtrack (because seeing her in satin short-shorts and roller skates was unquestionably the first time I felt the sick, helpless pangs of being in love) and playing guitar for Donna Summer (because the guitar solo on "Hot Stuff" is rad).

I would imagine that I was not in my bedroom, but up on stage in someplace huge, playing guitar behind Ms. Summer or Ms. Newton John before an audience composed entirely of girls from my second grade class. I was a phenom and no one had ever seen anything like me.

Reality, as is always the case with this particular disease, contradicted such whimsy.

I was born on December 16, 1973, the youngest of three children in what I always believed to be an upper-middle-class family, which I have since come to learn is simply a middle-class family with good credit. While both my parents are native Angelenos, they hardly fit the stereotype of the flighty Californian. They were too old to be hippies, as evidenced by their record collection, dominated by Petula Clark and Burt Bacharach. My father is a diligent, pragmatic man, having made his living in both commercial and residential real estate, while my mother was a homemaker with romantic hauntings from reading too much D. H. Lawrence in college.

The Family Williams was (and thankfully still is) typically dysfunctional; that is to say, my parents didn't really like each other, fought a lot, had affairs, and so forth, which led my brother (Paul, who is six years older than I), sister (Jennifer, nearly four years my senior), and me to embrace various neuroses. My brother took to booze and crashing cars into inanimate objects, my sister to a not very mild case of compulsive shopping, and me to existing almost entirely in an alternate universe in which I was a pop wunderkind.

The truth is that when these daydreams began keeping me up at night, I had no real musical identity, nor could I actually even play an instrument. During weekly visits to my Grandma Rene's house throughout my formative years, I would experiment with the electric organ she kept in her living room, but by no means could I play it. I was mesmerized by the keys that lit up to display the notes they represented, the foot pedals for deep bass notes, and cool drum rhythms like "Disco," "Samba," and the perennially popular "Fox Trot." Grandma Rene always had music laid out from the Mormon Tabernacle Choir, but I never saw her play any of it. Grandma Rene is evidence that my disease may be genetic, although her fantasy stage would have been specific to a tabernacle in Salt Lake City. I should point out that my family was not Mormon—my grandmother just dug their choir.

Like Grandma Rene, my fascination with music was limited to listening, and what I listened to as a child was what I was given. Believe it or not, the Donna Summer and Olivia Newton John cassettes weren't mine, but were pilfered from the glove box of my mom's '77 Mercury Monarch. In addition to Pop/Disco divas, I have fond memories of singing along with my mother to the Electric Light Orchestra's "Don't Bring Me Down" and ABBA's "Take a Chance on Me."

My first stab at forging my own musical identity was provided in the form of a gift certificate to Music Plus, the local record chain with an outlet near my home. Dressing me up in my finest pair of Tough Skins and a velvet Hang Ten shirt, my mom took my brother, sister, and me to the Orange Mall, where we spent hours sifting through rows of cassette tapes and LPs, until my brother appeared with two suggestions:

1. "Ghost in the Machine" by The Police on cassette.
2. The first Missing Persons EP on vinyl.

I knew nothing of either of these artists and these were, undoubtedly, albums that my brother planned on stealing from me as soon as we got home in one of his bedroom muggings. My mom, that peddler of disco, cautioned me against allowing him to tell me what to listen to, but needing the approval of my older brother, I assured her that these were indeed the albums I wanted.

When I got home and listened to them, I had no idea what to do with "Spirits in the Material World" or Missing Persons's "I Like Boys." By day's end, as designed, the albums ended up in my brother's possession.

I went on like this for some time, blindly sifting through my parents' collection of soft rock or the arena rock of Journey and Foreigner that my older siblings were enamored with, until I reached third grade and something happened.

Something wonderful.

Mötley Crüe's *Shout at the Devil* was given to me by a

classmate named John Gorski. He was a year older than I, but, because I had been placed in the combo class with fourth graders, so were most of my friends at that time. It was my access to that sophisticated world of elders that provided the precise element that would annihilate my ten-year-old world.

By the end of 1983, President Reagan was all over TV and in hard-hitting political news outlets like *People* magazine talking about Armageddon and various divinations for the end of the world. Like my musical choices up to this point, I was fed my politics by my parents, and they were avid supporters of the Great Communicator. I can't say we sat around talking about the looming Day of Judgment or anything, but when the man with his finger on the button is telling you that yours "may be the generation that sees Armageddon," it carries a little more weight than it does from, say, the homeless guy outside a Lakers game.

So when John Gorski handed me *Shout at the Devil*, in my mind, I had just been handed the soundtrack for the impending apocalypse.

First, there was the cover: four guys with teased hair who are wearing makeup are dressed in postapocalyptic leather outfits (complete with studded codpieces) and stand before hellish fire and smoke. On the inside are the titles and lyrics of songs like "God Bless the Children of the Beast" and little notes, such as "Caution: This record may contain backward messages." This was terrifying; lawsuits were pending against Judas Priest and Ozzy Osbourne for using subliminal messages to compel fans to commit suicide. I could hardly wait to listen.

And by no means as a side note here, there's the music itself. Each of the eleven tracks on the album features a chorus of vocals that sounds like an army on the march, chanting to the head-splitting rhythm of Tommy Lee doing things to a drum kit I had never heard before. The first song, "In the Beginning," is narrated by someone named Allister Fiend (who turned out to be bassist/songwriter Nikki Sixx doing a bad British accent, but I didn't know that then) and lays out a world that has been decimated by war and disease. Indeed, *Shout at the Devil* might be viewed as a concept album for Reagan's vision of the future.

With MTV, that vision went well beyond any album previously could. Like me, MTV was finding its identity in 1983 and was proving to be a culturally relevant promotional tool. While image has always been a big part of rock music (see Elvis, The Beatles, et al.), "look" was beginning to play a much more substantial role in our music choices as opposed to just the way an artist sounded. How else might you explain Culture Club?

Most of MTV was rather safe—artists and images that could be shown at 3:00 in the afternoon on basic cable without fear of recourse from the FCC. And then, like a revelation, among the barrage of Michael Jackson, Cyndi Lauper, Duran Duran, Lionel Richie, and even Taco's "Puttin' on the Ritz" (which, I have to admit, I sort of liked), appeared the video for "Looks that Kill," the third track off Mötley Crüe's album *Shout*.

It featured the Crüe in yet another post-end-of-the-world setting, corralling a herd of indigent, although sexy, women into a pen and performing the song for them in their leather battle gear. A devil woman, also very sexy, is summoned, and she is given great powers by the pentagram on Tommy Lee's bass drum. There is a scuffle between the devil woman and the Crüe, but ultimately they vanquish her in a puff of smoke, leaving behind only a burning pentagram.

As subtle as the imagery was, the whole *Shout at the Devil* experience fundamentally changed my musical DNA. It was forbidden, it was dirty, and it was visceral. This was not the poppy, over-produced Crüe of the late '80s that made *Dr. Feelgood;* you could smell the stink of drugs and STDs through the speakers on *Shout.* What the hell was David Byrne's talking head talking about in his oversized tweed suit when he kept saying, "Same as it ever was"? The Crüe didn't require such complex thought. They made my gut twinge in the same way that seeing the cover of one of my dad's *Playboy* magazines did. It was exactly what rock music for any generation is supposed to be: something that you hide from your parents because you're afraid of what they might think of you for listening to it. My parents would scoff at their hair, belittle their outfits, and say the music was just noise without taking a moment to consider the larger ramifications of the Crüe's music and image not only on society, but also on their youngest son.

For one thing, *Shout at the Devil* made me smoke my first cigarette. Gorski snaked a pack from his parents, and he and I hid behind some trees and lit up. Between noninhaling puffs, we talked about whether or not the Crüe actually were Satanists. They weren't encouraging us to shout *with* the Devil, you understand. They were saying shout *at* him. And who was the Devil, really? The Soviets? The Ayatollah Khomeini? Or was it Reagan himself? This conversation could only carry us so far, and my turn as pre-adolescent smoker was stunted when I was caught by my sister and a few other kids from the neighborhood who I was sure would run and tell my mother, whose wrath, it seemed to me then, might be greater than God's.

The other effect of *Shout* was to make me take the revolutionary step of learning to play an instrument. What was so tantalizing about the Crüe was the knowledge that they had been born of the clubs in Los Angeles, well within striking distance of my imagination. And as I soon discovered, there were dozens of these bands up there. For example, local act Ratt's "Round and Round" was receiving heavy rotation on MTV—as was W.A.S.P.

Just beyond the reach of my ten-year-old hands, a music scene was developing as rapidly as I was. This confluence of bands with big hair and outfits made of alternative fabrics might be chalked up to the large presence of record companies in the area or the glamour that is often associated with Southern California. But the answer, I believe, is much simpler.

They were all trying to re-create the success of the godfathers of So Cal Hair Metal: Van Halen.

While the local music scene was thriving with low-profile New Wave and punk bands like X and Black Flag, not since the hippies died had anything come out of Los Angeles that was as big as VH. Even before the success of their smash album *1984*, which, it should be noted, came out in 1983, they had sold more than 20 million albums and essentially saved the music world from a bleak future of soft rock, prog rock, and disco. They had big hair, wore Spandex and leather, and had the most original guitarist since Jimmy Paige as their namesake.

Their success attracted hordes of other bands to the area in hopes of emulating that success. The result was the birth of the Hollywood Scene, and Mötley Crüe was simply the next step in the evolution of that scene. While the Crüe couldn't match the musicianship of Van Halen (except Tommy Lee, who was simply ferocious), they would attract attention to themselves by making their hair bigger, throwing on some makeup, and dressing like extras in *Mad Max*. And with every band that came out of that scene, a hundred more popped up.

I figured I could be next. Indeed, the disease made me believe I was *destined* to be next. *Shout at the Devil* triggered the mutation that took my healthy fantasy and turned it into the sickness I still carry with me today.

My first instrument of choice was the piano, one reason being that I knew Eddie Van Halen began as a concert pianist. I thought perhaps the piano would reveal to me the fundamental genetic code of the Shred-a-saurus Rex I aspired to be. The larger reason for choosing the piano, though, was that my mom played it and we happened to have one in our family room. My mom's song was Beethoven's "Für Elise," which she played competently, although incessantly. To this day, any time my mother sits down at a piano, she plays "Für Elise" and nothing else.

She signed me up to take piano lessons from a quietly artistic woman named Mrs. Daisley, who gave lessons in her house just a few miles from my own. For an hour a week, she taught me how to read music, scales, and some simple songs. My tutelage was abbreviated, however, as someone broke into Mrs. Daisley's house one afternoon and raped her. She stopped teaching piano.

Upon entering El Rancho Junior High School in my twelfth year, I joined the concert band, choosing tenor and alto saxophone somewhat arbitrarily. But if you're going to join the school band, sax or percussion is totally the way to go.

We spent most of our time rehearsing for seasonal concerts that our parents felt obligated to attend. It wasn't that we were that bad, but I'm sure the last thing my father wanted to do when he got back from his two-hour commute was sit in a junior high school cafeteria in an uncomfortable metal folding chair while a group of twelve- and thirteen-year-olds honked, screeched, and wheezed their way through "Jingle Bell Rock" at Christmas time and "Peter Gunn" in the spring.

That he did at all is a testament to how nurturing both my parents were of my creative pursuits. Being unfamiliar with the symptoms of the disease, they couldn't have predicted how far I would try to take it. So for Christmas that year, they gave me a Casio keyboard.

That morning, under the still-glowing Christmas tree, I wrote my first full musical composition. It was a waltz. It didn't have a name (waltzes seldom do), nor did it contain any saxophone or satanic imagery, but it did effectively expose my rock star fantasy and began my slow dance (a waltz, I suppose) toward the realization that the whole thing would have been better left in my head.

The reviews of that first waltz were mixed.

"That's great, honey!"—Mom and Dad
"Mom, tell Craigy to shut up!"—My sister
"You're a fag."—My brother

What encouragement I did get post-waltz inspired me to continue experimenting, perhaps in another time signature. After the Christmas tree was removed, I had to find some other suitable location to compose, so I took it upon myself to establish my first recording studio.

The playroom was what my family called the long room in the front part of the house that ran above the garage. It was where I had a bumper pool table, a closet full of board games, and my InTellivision, which, after Atari, was one of the earliest home gaming systems. Now, with a dual cassette deck boombox next to the speaker of my Casio, it was my own Electric Ladyland.

I had written another song, this one in a much more aspiring-rock-star-approved 4:4 time signature. Once everyone in my family tired of listening to me play it, I decided to open the doors of my studio to outsiders and invited over my first audience.

The only interested party was a kid who lived down the street from me, a young man who, as destiny would have it, shared in my sickness and, before we'd finish high school, would become the greatest frontman in the history of the Anaheim Hills/Yorba Linda area.

Kid Ego

The truth of the matter is, the further I get away from it, the harder it is to remember what the truth of the matter is. So when I say that Tyler Jacobs was a sociopath, I mean only that, as I look back on it now, he seemed to derive pleasure from hurting other people emotionally. I'm no psychologist, nor do I wish to delve into that rather interpretive science, but I don't think I'd be going too far out on a limb to suggest that his mother's suicide had something to do with it.

Colleen Jacobs was found on the floor of the guest room of her four-bedroom home in Anaheim Hills, having taken an overdose of sleeping pills. Her daughter, Tanya, who was ten years Tyler's senior (and had been on a blind date with Warrant frontman Jani Lane), arrived at the house for a scheduled lunch and discovered the body, face down, in a small pool of blood. Mrs. Jacobs's nose was broken when her body fell from the bed after rigor mortis set in. Accompanying the cadaver was a note holding Tyler's "attitude" partly responsible for her decision.

To be fair, my knowledge of Tyler's relationship with his mother is limited to the following:

- Colleen gave birth to Tyler on July 13, 1974.

- When Tyler was eleven, Colleen and Tyler's father, Glen, divorced. Colleen made Tyler see a shrink, who gave him books he never read about coping with his parents' divorce.

- Colleen gave Tyler Van Halen's *1984* LP for his birthday.

- Colleen started dating a man who drove a white Ford Taurus.

- Colleen told Tyler that, when she died, she wanted to be buried in a hamburger box. Tyler told her it would have to be a box for the Whaler, the now-extinct Burger King fish sandwich.

- Tyler rubbed frozen yogurt on Colleen's boyfriend's white Ford Taurus door handle and he got mad.

- Colleen and white Ford Taurus broke up.

- Colleen killed herself and left a note holding Tyler's attitude partly responsible.

There may have been other events that informed their relationship to which I wasn't privy. Whatever these events might or might not have been, however, I can't imagine there was anything Tyler could have done to warrant such an emotional holocaust.

Exacerbating the problem, undoubtedly, was the fact that Tyler was spoiled to no end. Tyler's father, Glen, was the principal at an alternative high school. While Glen worked with troubled youth daily, his solution to the events of Tyler's formative years was to give the kid whatever he wanted: sports equipment, toys, and, as the band became the priority, a set of drums, microphones, a rock star wardrobe—pretty much anything he (or, often I) wanted. When we needed a place to rehearse, Glen agreed to park his car in the driveway so that we could take over the garage with our amplifiers, drum kits, and reverie.

Tyler was also the kid who was good at almost anything he tried, and no one was more aware of this fact than Tyler himself. The youngest member of the band, he was witty, good-looking, an outstanding athlete, and almost mythical in bed, a sort of sexual unicorn.

The result was a young man with a well-developed ego. It became a source of humor for the rest of the band, and he eventually earned the nickname Kid Ego after the song you've probably never heard of by Extreme.

Yet Tyler's supreme confidence made him the perfect frontman. He was oblivious to the absurdity of his actions, which is necessary for anyone in lace gloves. For a good rock 'n' roll frontman, singing is secondary. What matters is charisma. Most frontmen would describe themselves as "vocalists" as opposed to "singers." David Lee Roth doesn't sing in the way that, say, Aretha Franklin does. But I'd like to see the Queen of Soul scream like Diamond

Dave does in "Atomic Punk" while doing a karate kick off a drum riser.

What the frontman lacks in vocal precision, he makes up for in what is known as "stage presence." Such presence ranges from the rudimentary (for example, pacing while pointing a finger at the balcony, holding hands with multiple members of the front row, or throwing an arm around another band member) to the expert (which incorporates moves from the worlds of martial arts, gymnastics, and interpretive dance).

Stage presence is a kind of energy that you should observe only from a distance (usually while holding a plastic cup filled with some sort of alcohol) and with multicolored lights flashing down from above. Because spending time away from the stage with a frontman is like playing kickball with a land mine, which is why the best frontmen of the Hair Metal era were either kicked out of their band (Diamond Dave/Van Halen), left their band (Sebastian Bach/Skid Row), or fired everyone in the band and kept the band name (Axl Rose/Guns N' Roses).

Tyler had the same kind of energy, albeit to a far lesser extent than the supernovas listed above. Still, to watch the same kid with whom I played Little League baseball, street football, and "kick the can" get to the point where he could spit water over the front row of girls at The Roxy Theater was astounding. But any jerk could do it. To then witness the same girls throw their heads back in what I think was ecstasy and rub the water into their skin made him a rock star. It was validation of his ego, and he used that as a kind of currency with which to influence the rest of us, first in terms of our sound, then our image, and, ultimately, our behavior.

I didn't know any of this, of course, when I invited Tyler over to my playroom to listen to my latest Casio composition. Tyler Jacobs was simply my best friend, because you have best friends when you're twelve, and who better to invite over to hear my masterpiece?

The song was a slow number, what might be called a power ballad, with a simple four-chord bass line and a circular three-note melody. As Tyler listened to me play it, that stage presence welled up, and his normally innocent face took on an almost pained look. His eyes closed, his cheeks filled with color, and the veins and muscles in his neck became taut.

Inexplicably, he just started singing.

I must emphasize that, up to this point, singing was not something Tyler and I did together. Outside of musicals and certain animated feature films, I don't think breaking into song is something that generally happens in the "real world." I would suggest, therefore, that we dismiss any construct of this "real world" because from that moment, we were no longer functioning in it.

My initial reaction was one of embarrassment, both by him and for him. All I could figure was, with all he'd been through, maybe the kid just needed a way to express himself. After a few times through the chord progression, though, my embarrassment began to ebb, and I came to see that Tyler and I were kindred spirits, sharers of a common disease. Besides, he wasn't that bad. The rock star fantasy world now had *two* inhabitants.

At the end of the song, which was only determined by the cessation of his vocals (I was already losing creative control, you see), we simply stared at each other, nodding. I grabbed a blank tape and popped it in the tape deck. "Let's try it again."

We did, each time toying with the lyrics, adding a keyboard solo, until we got just the right version of it down on tape.

It was order from chaos. It was something from nothing. It was spontaneous.

It was "Sun Angel."

Before I reveal the lyrics, I would like to point out two things.

1. We were twelve.
2. We weren't nearly as talented as the previous passage suggests we were.

Regardless, the initial result follows as such:

VERSE

It was late on a Friday night
We were all tired
But then I met you
I knew you were
The one to spend
My life with
And make all the darkness turn to light

I realize that last line may seem like a mouthful relative to the rest of the composition. It was.

'Cause you're my sun angel
Flying in the wind
Someday we will be together as one
My sun angel
Stay with me

The song was a big hit with my mom, of course, but more surprisingly with my older sister. I suppose my sister was our first groupie, as it became clear that she saw "Ty," as she called him quite suddenly, in a whole new light.

With such positive reaction on a domestic audience, we decided to test the waters of a broader market. The following Monday, we took the tape to school and played it on Tyler's Walkman for some of the girls during the fifteen-minute break between second and third period known as "Nutrition." The girls stood in a circle in a crowded hallway, one at a time putting the headphones to their ears and giggling. Giggling, as far as we were concerned, was better than outright laughter.

"Who is it?" they asked after they had time to discuss it among themselves.

Ah, how to refer to the composers of "Sun Angel"? Certainly, the name had to follow the rule of any mid-1980s hard rock band: a severe-sounding adjective preceding a usually pedestrian noun to make it sound medieval, satanic, or in some way belonging to an insane asylum. Iron Maiden. Mötley Crüe. Twisted Sister . . .

". . . Stone Claw," we told them, nonchalant, chomping on Munchos and Funions or some other "nutritional" food source.

"We like it," they told us, and they then disappeared back to the giggling and mystifying world of thirteen-year-old girls.

With a growing fan base and the support of our loving families, we thus returned to the playroom with the intent of writing more songs. We figured we could have an entire album recorded by the end of the year, sell a few million copies of it, and be retired by the time our voices changed. But we were never able to write any other songs, so we just played "Sun Angel" over and over. And over.

It was my "Für Elise."

I soon discovered that the solo I had written between the final choruses might sound better on a guitar. Fortunately, there was a Yamaha acoustic that was collecting dust in the hall closet, a remnant of my older brother's long-abandoned attempt at becoming KISS.

"But Craig, how did you learn to play the guitar so quickly?" you might ask. To which I can only respond: It wasn't much of a guitar solo. Still, there could be nothing more in tune with my rock star fantasy than a guitar solo. Nothing, that is, except the gift I received from my parents for my thirteenth birthday.

A "Flying-V" electric guitar. White, pearl inset on the neck, dude, a fucking Flying-V. While I never explicitly asked for a Flying-V, I was, at that time, obsessed with Ozzy's *Tribute* album, the cover of which features the Oz holding up his late guitarist, Randy Rhodes, who in turn embraces his polka-dotted Flying-V. I can only assume my parents saw this and decided that must be my dream guitar. They turned out to be correct.

I have heard that in certain theocracies around the world, it is forbidden to display some guitars in storefronts because their shape too much resembles that of a woman. Clearly, these governments are in touch with their inner pubescent boy, because I stared at this guitar and fantasized about touching it almost as much as I played it.

Eventually, I signed on for lessons at the Music Maker, the local music store and place of musical learning. My instructor was a long-haired chap who wore leather vests and seemed exasperated by my passion for Hair Metal.

Regardless, he taught me how to play "Ain't Talkin' 'Bout Love" and "Suicide Solution." I began spending my evenings hunkered next to my stereo, listening to KNAC, trying to figure out more songs on my own. I became fairly adept at learning to play songs by ear, but if there were any jams that were beyond me, I'd take a tape to Mr. Music Maker, who'd sigh and begrudgingly teach them to me.

As I improved on the guitar and the Casio collected dust, however, a new problem presented itself. At this point, Stone Claw was a keyboard-centric outfit. Like Van Halen's "Jump," "Sun Angel" was a keyboard song, and any attempts to transfer it to the guitar were met with failure. Yet there was little chance I would set aside my Flying-V to conceal myself behind a keyboard. As a result, Stone Claw came to a landmark decision.

We needed a keyboard player.

☰ 3 ☰

Way Kul Junior

Devolution in my playroom, 1988. Once my mom made that banner,
we were stuck with the name.

Sunil Gupta was an Indian boy whom Tyler and I called
Sonny because we are Caucasian and as a culture do that
to "foreign" names.

Sonny was the oldest of three kids in the Gupta clan,
and the only son of his father, Kul (pronounced like the
Kool brand of cigarettes), who, along with his wife, Lak-
shmi, emigrated from India to the United States. Kul made
this move as a young man to pursue an education in engi-
neering at the University of Michigan. Sonny was born
shortly thereafter in the Motor City on April 3, 1974.
Within a few years, the Gupta family packed up and moved

to Southern California so that Kul could pursue work in the region's massive aerospace and defense industries.

Kul was diminutive, no more than five and a half feet tall, and bald, but he had a convincing smile and smarts. With his knowledge not only of how to build bombs, but also how to deliver them, it was only natural that Kul would eventually become the band's first manager. Kul was a natural salesman—a charming South Asian Colonel Tom Parker. Yet he was also avuncular, the dad in the group who told us dirty jokes, taught us magic tricks, took us on weekend ski trips up to the local mountains, and slipped us our first sips of beer. Kul constructed a wooden half-pipe in his front yard so all the neighborhood kids had a place to skate. He also kept a '78 burnt orange Corvette Stingray with T-tops in his driveway, and would occasionally allow Sonny or me to move it from the curb to the driveway. Kul was oblivious to the idea of generational gaps—he simply wanted to be a part of his son's life.

Eventually, he became an integral part of mine, too. Sonny's family was a second family to me, inviting me over for dinners and family functions. They taught me a few words and phrases in Marathi, then giggled and shook their heads when I'd try to repeat them. I got to know aunts, uncles, and grandparents who visited from around the world and learned a very important fact about Sonny's family.

The Guptas were almost neurotically successful. Even seemingly feeble grandmothers had multiple graduate degrees in biology, economics, or sociology. Sonny's youngest sister was a sort of genius gymnast while his other sister was that homecoming-queen/student-body-president/key club sweetheart/Miss Anaheim Hills type, what college admissions boards and high school boys would call "well rounded," although for different reasons.

As a result, an inordinate amount of pressure was placed on Sonny to succeed at anything he did, be it the academic decathlon, playing soccer, or jamming out in a rock band with his friends. I distinctly remember Sonny coming home with a 4.0 on his report card only to be told by his mother, in her brittle, Marathi accent, "Only 4.0? You are bum, Sonny."

The pressures of being a Gupta never affected Sonny in an adverse way—they simply motivated him to separate himself from the herd. Needless to say, this is exactly the kind of guy you want in your rock 'n' roll army if you plan on taking over the world.

Our newest lieutenant played clarinet in the El Rancho Junior High concert band. First chair. I had met Sonny in fourth grade, when both of us were required to transfer from our respective elementary schools to Imperial Elementary for Gifted and Talented Education, or G.A.T.E.

The school segregated the "gifted" kids from the "regular" kids, as the administration referred to the sadly ungifted students, ensuring that recess was spent having to defend ourselves from said "regular" kids, whose bodies typically had developed quicker than their brains. They would call us names like "Stupid G.A.T.E.," and when we'd try to explain to them that their derogatory term was an oxymoron, they would punch us, usually somewhere in the gut region.

Being one of the few persons of color in our class, Sonny was even an exile among the geeky outcasts. When we'd play "The A-Team" at recess, he was always B. A. Baracus because he was the closest thing to a black mohawked man we had. I, incidentally, was Murdock, the crazy one, because, with half my life spent fantasizing about being a rock star, I was the closest thing to a schizophrenic we had.

When kids endure that kind of hardship together, as Sonny and I did, a bond is naturally formed. It also reinforced in us the idea that we weren't like other kids, and it made us do things like try to start our own magazines, write computer programs, or, since we weren't interested in/good at any of those other things, form rock bands. We were geeks, to be sure, but we saw starting our own rock band as our bid for membership into the world of cool.

And what's cooler than a clarinetist?

In addition to his woodwind, Sonny happened to have an even nicer Casio than I had (more drum beats, you understand) and he could play the harpsichord solo (using the harpsichord function on his Casio) from The Beatles's song "In My Life." And if we ever needed a clarinet solo, like Van Halen's on "Big Bad Bill (Is Sweet William Now)" off the *Diver Down* album, we were set.

Tyler and Sonny didn't really know each other all that well, as Tyler wasn't in any of the honors classes Sonny and I were automatically put into in junior high as G.A.T.E. alum. Yet I had provided Sonny with a glowing enough recommendation that Tyler acquiesced and a new member was initiated into the fantasy world.

* * *

With a new lineup, Stone Claw realized it was time for reinvention: a reexamination of our band philosophy and, without question, a new band name. With a Hindu brought into the fold, and I will swear to this until my dying day, my first recommendation for a new name was Nirvana, but it was rejected on the grounds that it was too weird. So instead, I opened up the dictionary one afternoon and found an even better name. In fact, the word seemed to spread across the entire page:

Devolution

Many of our critics, I'm sure, will point out that there happened to be a band already called Devolution, more commonly known as Devo. What those critics fail to realize, though, is the fact that I had told my mom about the name and she promptly had a red vinyl banner made with the name "Devolution" stenciled across in white, so we were stuck with it.

Now all we needed were some more songs.

We were finally able to come up with a tune called "In the Dark" that was essentially "Sun Angel" in reverse. But if we threw one in the beginning of a set and the other near the end, no one was going to notice.

Still, two songs a set did not make, so we started performing covers. "Wild Thing," of course, because it was so simple even a stand-up comedian like Sam Kinison could perform it. ("Wild Thing" was eliminated from our set after we saw a band on the Strip who altered the lyrics to "Wild bitch/You make my balls itch.") "In My Life" because we couldn't let Sonny's solo go to waste. And we always closed with "Sun Angel."

For his thirteenth birthday in that summer of 1987, Tyler got a drum kit, a dark-red Pearl five-piece set that he played well enough. We set up in the playroom, hanging Christmas lights for ambiance, and hung the Devolution banner on the wall behind us to create a makeshift stage. We'd rehearse our set to an audience comprised of pillows and obsolete video games, pretending we were in the arenas we saw in Mötley Crüe's "Home Sweet Home" video, the original live concert music video, and the one by which all others must be judged, even Poison's commendable "Every Rose Has Its Thorn."

Finally, while the Flying-V looked kick-ass, it actually fell out of tune fairly easily, and would never last through the rigors of an entire set, even in rehearsal. So I withdrew a few hundred dollars from the savings account my grandparents had started for me and contributed to every birthday and Christmas, and I insisted that my father take me down to the Guitar Center so that I could buy my first Fender Stratocaster. While the Strat is not necessarily indigenous to the butt rock community, I had seen Def Leppard's Steve Clark, aka The Riffmaster, playing one in the "Love Bites" video, so it was good enough for me.

My Strat was red and white, almost identical to the color combination of Tyler's drum kit, as well as the Devolution banner my mom had purchased for us. The combination of the instruments, the color coordination, and the energy ready to explode from my parents' playroom meant that all we needed was a human audience to bear witness.

We invited some girls over, a group of young ladies Sonny and I had known since the G.A.T.E. years, who also happened to be in the El Rancho concert band. There was Tracy (French horn, whose father was also teacher/conductor of the El Rancho concert band), Stacy (clarinet), Lisa (French horn), Tina (clarinet), and Sarena, who I don't think played any instrument but was fantasy-satisfyingly cute.

They sat on the sectional against the wall while Devolution took the stage. The three of us dressed in denim and high-tops, on account of the fact that, at that time, I didn't know where to find the postapocalyptic fashion of the Crüe and Twisted Sister. Even if I did, I'm not sure my mom would have taken me leather shopping. That would have deviated from the Gotcha pastel pants and Town & Country T-shirts she had grown accustomed to buying for me. Acid-washed jeans with the legs pegged at the ankle, it seemed to me, were a reasonable compromise.

Devolution performed for these girls for thirty minutes or so, with the initial duties being Tyler on drums, Sonny on keyboard, and me on guitar and vocals. I wasn't much of a singer, but I thought I could mumble the words to "Wild Thing" just as well as the next guy. Granted, the girls laughed at us while we were performing, and my mom sneaking in to snap photos didn't help our image. All the same, the set came to a rousing conclusion with a performance of "Sun Angel," with Tyler taking the fore-ground and me moving to the back with Sonny, his Casio taking on drum duties.

When the gig concluded to the sound of five girls clapping, playfully egging us on with calls for an encore (we didn't know any more songs at this point), we all walked down to a nearby park where a miraculous thing happened:

The girls made out with us.

Well, some of us.

Okay, one of them made out with Tyler.

Regardless, the revelatory nature of this development cannot be overstated. While the El Rancho Junior High concert band met certain elective requirements toward my commencement to high school, the class never provided an opportunity whereupon girls waited to put themselves into compromising situations with me afterward, despite the fact that I played the sexiest instrument and could even play the bleating sax riff from the Beastie Boys's "Brass Monkey."

Being in a rock band, however, led to simple cause and effect. We play a few songs, one of us gets to make out with a girl. Maybe next time, all of us would. I wish I could say that, at the age of thirteen, I had aspirations beyond this, but, alas, that was not the case.

So we did it again a month or so later and got the same results. On and on it went for months, with us holding concerts in the playroom for the same five or six girls, "Sun Angel" acting as our anchor, Tyler getting to make out with one of the girls, and Sonny and I looking on expectantly. It occurred to me then that I might take it upon myself to go solo and try this newfound aphrodisiac without Tyler there to get in the way.

One Friday night, a friend brought his girlfriend, who lived down the hill from me (Anaheim Hills has many hills, if nothing less), over to my house while my parents were out. I immediately took them both up to my room, popped a tape into my stereo, and played along to Van Halen's version of "You Really Got Me." I chose the Flying-V over the Strat for purposes of aesthetics, and it apparently worked. The next night, this young lady invited me to sneak out and meet her down by the community pool.

She was my girlfriend until the following weekend, when she came over and Tyler joined me for a jam session in my bedroom. As he sang along to my guitar, in his closed-eyed, impassioned, frontman way, I simply became Tyler's accompaniment and, later that night, she became Tyler's girlfriend. I was quickly learning one of the indisputable truths of the rock star world: Vocalists get all the ass.

There was no denying, however, that Tyler was infinitely more comfortable singing than I was. Not only was he better at it than I, he was a natural frontman. He was dramatic: gesturing to the crowd (even if there only were five of them), throwing his head back, closing his eyes, and holding up two fists, as though there really were a sun angel flying in the wind and someday they *would* be together as one. He actually liked to sing. Whether or not he was good is irrelevant; he believed he was.

The only problem was, when Tyler would come out to sing "Sun Angel" during our playroom gigs, we had to revert to the synthesized drumbeat on Sonny's Casio. This was no good. This was not rock. This was not cool. We were not fucking Depeche Mode.

And so Tyler introduced us to Kyle Siegel.

4

No Room for Emotion

Kyle Siegel lost his virginity in the Camp Snoopy section of Knott's Berry Farm.

Nestled in the northern Orange County hamlet of Buena Park, Knott's is at the end of Beach Boulevard, just beyond the Medieval Times Dinner Theater and the Ripley's Believe It or Not Museum's satellite campus. It is Knott's Berry Farm, however, that stands as the real attraction here, as it is allegedly the world's first theme park. In addition to roller coasters and hopeful actors disguised as cowboys, they are quite well known for their foodstuffs, which are sold in markets worldwide. Perhaps you have tasted their jellies?

Between 1987 and 1989, Tyler, Kyle, and sometimes Sonny and I would have our parents drop us off at Knott's on Friday evenings, not for the delicious chicken you can purchase at their country store, but because of Cloud 9, an all-ages club within the amusement park's confines.

Cloud 9 attracted primarily a goth crowd, teenagers dressed in black trench coats and Doc Martens, with ratty black hair, all in contrast to their stark, pale faces, hidden under a cake of white foundation, eyeliner, and, often, lipstick. Being among the depressed throngs of The Cure, The Smiths, and Bauhaus fans may seem an odd haven for guys who were soon to become Hair Metal gods most comfortable discussing why Guns N' Roses was infinitely superior to L.A. Guns (it started with the soul of Slash), but Cloud 9 was (a) the only all-ages club we knew of and (b) close enough for our parents to drive us to without too much of a fight.

That it was a goth hangout only added to our amusement. There was something inherently funny about a kid dressed up like Robert Smith from The Cure enjoying a late-night churro and a Pepsi. Why, we mused, would hordes of privileged kids from sunny Orange County associate themselves with the general gloom of industrial northern England? Perhaps the only one of the four of us who might have related to the goth movement was Kyle.

Kyle was born on the Ides of March, 1974, to Ari and Connie Siegel. I'm not exactly sure what Ari did, aside from eat dairy desserts from the carton and frozen hot dogs from the AM/PM mini-mart. Apparently, his job had something to do with buying cars at repo auctions and then selling them for a profit, so that the Siegels always had some car disintegrating in front of their house.

Connie Siegel was defined by her hair, not in the

manner of early Andre Agassi, but more in the way of Tom Kiefer, lead singer of Cinderella. It was spectacular in both size and ambition. Connie sometimes sold real estate, taking clients out in whichever Cadillac Ari had secured that month, while in her lap sat Kasha, her white Pomeranian. The only thing she loved more than that dog was Kyle's older brother, Marty.

Marty was at least seven years older than us, lived at home, and was constantly taking showers. Every time I came by the Siegel house, Marty would answer the door with his hairy cantaloupe belly hanging over the towel wrapped around his waist. Marty was into The Pixies and Mojo Nixon (Mojo even called him at home a few times), and it seemed he was put on Earth to harass his little brother for liking shitty music.

If you put a bird in the Antarctic, over time its wings become flippers and its feathers become waxy; it loses its ability to fly, and it becomes a penguin. Upon returning from the zero gravity environs of space, astronauts have weak hearts that have to reacclimate to the gravitational pull of Earth. And, when you give a young man a father like Ari, a mother like Connie, and a brother like Marty, the apparent manifestation is an exasperating stutter.

It was a constant nuisance for Kyle. He took speech classes, went to a therapist, smoked, but nothing helped. When he called, you knew it was him because there was always a thick silence as his tongue rolled around helplessly in his mouth, until finally you'd hear, "Wwwwwhat's up?" Kyle was extremely bright, a whiz at math, and his approach to the stutter was equally calculated. You felt sorry for him, and he knew it.

Unfortunately, Kyle played drums the way he spoke; he was always just a half-beat behind. His strength may have also been his weakness: He had a black Tama drum kit with two bass drums. While it looked cool on stage, it was simply too much temptation. His beats were confused, inconsistent, a cacophony of bass drums, cowbells, snares, hi-hats, tom-toms, ride, crash, and splash symbols. Sometimes it sounded more like someone was knocking the kit over rather than actually playing it.

But Lars Ulrich from Metallica had two bass drums, as did Randy Castillo from Ozzy's band. So naturally Kyle had to have two, too. Besides, he had longish hair, he smoked, and he listened to the Crüe.

So he was in.

And so it came to pass that, when we hit our mid-teen years and finally realized what we were supposed to do with the erections that had been tormenting us for the previous three or four years, Kyle learned to use his stutter to his advantage. He could say essentially anything and it would come off as innocuous, almost charming.

And it wasn't Kyle's appearance that did it for him. He certainly wasn't unattractive, but he also didn't have the kind of handsome suave that would allow him to say something like "Nnnnnnnnice tits, c-c-can I see 'em?" without suffering a punch to the gut. He looked something like former *SNL* cast member Jon Lovitz: brown hair, brown eyes, and a nose that dominated his face. He also had the early ability to grow a decent amount of facial hair.

Picking up girls was an art form for Kyle, not because he was necessarily good at it, but because the more nervous he got, the more effective he was. It was like a kid in a wheelchair challenging you to a fight. He was the aggressor, and yet the girls felt sympathy for him. And sympathy is a bizarre, albeit potent, aphrodisiac.

To understand what Kyle brought to the band when he joined in the early part of 1988, we must briefly leap forward in time, to the winter of 1989, when the exchange that led to Kyle's loss of innocence in Camp Snoopy was initiated.

Because I was a few months older than everyone else in the band, I was first to receive my driver's license. It was a big coup the first time I was able to drive Tyler and Kyle to Knott's. As usual, we made our way to Cloud 9 and moved through the crowd of black-clad teens dancing to "Bela Lugosi's Dead."

Kyle had previously met this young lady, whom I'll call Sara (not because I'm trying to protect her, but because I have no idea what her name is). While Tyler and I stood in the corner, sipping Sprite, nodding our heads, trying to fit in by wearing black mock turtlenecks, Kyle hit on Sara. There was a lot of hugging and laughing before Kyle walked over to Tyler and me to suggest that we all go back to my car and drive around a bit. Because that's fun at that age.

While Tyler sat shotgun, Kyle rode in back with Sara, each attempting desperately to swallow the other's face. We smoked cigarettes, listened to Faster Pussycat's magnificent debut cassette tape, and drove up and down Beach Boulevard. Tyler and I had adjusted the fader on the stereo so that the speakers were blasting "No Room for Emotion" only in the backseat, which had a dual effect.

First, when Kyle and Sara spoke, they had to practically shout, and, second, Tyler and I didn't have Taime Downe's voice cackling in our ears so that we could hear everything Kyle and Sara hollered at each other.

After several minutes of incessant slobbering, Kyle pulled away, and I could actually hear his tongue rolling around in his mouth. Presently, he was able to articulate his deepest emotions.

"Head?"

I heard one sharp feminine giggle, followed by "What?"

Again, Kyle made a series of odd clicking noises, a lingual conflict, but he then finally erupted with "Suck my dick?"

In the front, there was quiet celebration, the shared look of raised eyebrows and a grin that agreed to maintain silence.

In the back, however, there was much negotiation to be done. While most young men would get a slap in the face or at least a "Fuck off, pull the car over," Kyle received a quiet "But your friends are in the front seat" and a soft kiss on the neck. I have no doubt that her reaction had everything to do with the stutter.

"So what? They won't notice."

"I don't know . . ."

"Just rrrrreal quick. Like," I thought he might swallow his own tongue here, "ffffive minutes."

There was a pause, then, "Two minutes."

I'm pretty sure I heard Kyle smile as her head disappeared into his lap. I looked over my shoulder to see Kyle, a suddenly enlightened figure, an erotic Buddha, legs spread, eyes closed, smile on his face. He must have felt me looking because he opened his eyes, smiled broader, and waved at me.

I lit up another cigarette and continued to drive up and down Beach Boulevard. I pulled through the Del Taco drive-through for a Mr. Pibb and a spicy chicken quesadilla, Kyle waving happily to the speechless cashier as we drove away.

After a few minutes, Sara stopped.

Click, click, pop, click, "Wwwwhy'd you stop?"

"We should get out of the car."

Without hesitation, "Craig, pull over, dude."

When I did, we were back by Knott's, just outside Camp Snoopy. Because it was the children's section of the park, it shut down much earlier than the rest of Knott's. Kyle and Sara hopped out and disappeared into orange light and shadows.

I don't know what happened in Camp Snoopy, of course, but I imagine, while Tyler and I waited in the car and listened to the entirety of the "B" side of Faster Pussycat's cassette, that Kyle lay Sara down inside some exaggerated dog house on top of which, during the day, some guy in a Snoopy costume pretended to write WWI flying ace stories on an old typewriter, and fornicated.

I do know that Kyle Siegel entered Camp Snoopy speaking a stuttering English the *Peanuts* kids could at least understand and left speaking the incomprehensible *Wah wah wah wah wah* of manhood.

5

I Wanna Rock!

Me with my Flying-V, 1986.

What is it that inspires a fourteen-year-old boy to write songs?

Many artists cite a higher power as the source of their talents. George Frideric Handel, for example, refused to take payment for any of his performances because he believed he was merely a vessel for the message of God. But Handel wrote "The Messiah." He composed music that has lasted centuries. If inspiration really involves supernatural influence that qualifies men to receive and communicate divine truth, were the gods just going through a tough time at the end of the 1980s? Did God inspire the lyrics of Warrant frontman Jani Lane?

Sing, O Muse! Of a cherry pie and how it might serve as a metaphor of the female pudendum.

Literally, the word *inspire* signifies breathing in that which is around you, and by 1988, the music world had been seized by big-haired, leather-clad warriors, having nothing but a good time whilst pouring sugar all over themselves.

Hair Metal had exploded onto the mainstream, moving from late night and weekend rotations on MTV's *Head-banger's Ball* to heavy afternoon rotation, beginning in 1986 with the release of Bon Jovi's *Slippery When Wet*. With megahits such as "You Give Love a Bad Name," "Wanted Dead or Alive," and, perhaps the single most popular song of the era, "Livin' on a Prayer," *Slippery When Wet* took Hair Metal out of the cellar and created a rump rock hysteria. Although bands like Quiet Riot and Twisted Sister had previously enjoyed much in the way of commercial success, *Slippery When Wet* was a manicured, smiling version of Hair Metal that was previously un-known. It was clean cut and radio friendly—the Bing Crosby to *Shout at the Devil*'s Little Richard.

Suddenly MTV and Top 40 radio were inundated with bands with big hair: Poison, Cinderella, Ratt, Lita Ford, Winger, Britny Fox, Vixen, Bulletboys, KIX-S, Dangerous Toys, Damn Yankees, Bad English, Tesla, Firehouse, Great White, Whitesnake, White Lion . . . Oh my!

These were groups that were using the same elements

the Crüe had on *Shout* (makeup, leather, big hair), but gone was any sense of danger or rebellion. The world of suffering and chaos that had been foretold on *Shout* and the possible apocalypse once mentioned by President Reagan were distant memories by 1988, replaced by the optimism of an economic boom and the imminent collapse of the Evil Empire. Hair Metal paid homage to that optimism in the form of neon, Spandex, and massive amounts of cocaine. Even original Hair Metal gods like Def Leppard and the Crüe polished up their acts with their respective albums *Hysteria* and *Girls, Girls, Girls,* and they saw a new level of success as a result.

Despite the globalization of what was now officially being called Glam Metal, also known in some corners as Hair Metal, butt rock, cock rock, or rump rock, the capital of the ass-rocking (almost forgot to mention that one) nation remained Los Angeles. In addition to the reemergence of the Crüe, Poison was the next step in the (d)evolution of the Hollywood metal scene. They were even more lackluster musicians than Mötley Crüe (again, I exempt Tommy Lee from any such criticism; he played upside-down drum solos from a steel cage while wearing nothing more than a leather bikini!), and they successfully diverted attention from this fact by wearing even more makeup, making their hair even bigger, and wearing even more absurd clothing. The result was an acceptably bawdy act that produced several Top 40 hits, including "Every Rose Has Its Thorn," which, by the end of 1988, hit number one and effectively kept my own rock 'n' roll fantasy alive.

Of all the bands to crawl their way out of the local

music scene in 1988, however, none was more inspirational than the Michelangelos of the Hair Metal genre, Guns N' Roses, and their Sistine Chapel of an album, *Appetite for Destruction*.

GNR were the antithesis of the pretty, radio friendly acts surrounding them. Released in the early part of 1987, *Appetite*'s first single, "Welcome to the Jungle," didn't immediately catch on. It was frightening music: part punk, part blues, and part metal. The video contained disturbing images of a lanky, strung-out kid with teased-out red hair being strapped to a chair in a straitjacket and forced to watch violent images on TV.

It wasn't until the almost charming "Sweet Child O' Mine" was released that the GNR assault began. The song spent three weeks at number one during the summer of '88 and was followed up by "Paradise City," and by the time I entered my freshman year of high school that fall, seemingly every kid in Southern California was wearing a bandana around his head and doing the Axl Rose snake dance.

Somehow, my musical idols had also become the heroes of the "regular" kids. And rather than being territorial of my heroes and their songs, I saw it as an opportunity to finally be accepted. Once my classmates saw that I was just as cool as the guys they listened to on the radio and watched on MTV, the entirety of the Orange Unified School District would worship me for the metal god that I, too, had become.

While I was a freshman at Canyon High School, my sister was a senior, which meant that other students knew who I was and didn't terrorize me the way they might other freshmen. Despite being uninvolved in student government, athletics, or anything that might be considered academic, my sister was immensely popular in high school. She ran with the party girls, who spent most of their nights floating from kegger to kegger, often hosting them at our house when our parents were out of town. Screw with Jenny Williams's little brother and you might not find yourself welcome at the next Canyon High social event.

There were other benefits as well. That fall, I was taken to my first concert by a young man who wanted to hook up with my sister's best friend. He was a year or two out of high school, and to demonstrate his suaveness, he ordered up a limo to take my sister, her friend, and me to see The Scorpions at the Irvine Meadows Amphitheater as part of their Savage Amusement tour.

Since I was a big fan of The Scorps, particularly their power ballad "Winds of Change," a political number about the slowly crumbling Soviet regime (not to mention that I liked their classics such as "Rock You Like a Hurricane" and "Still Loving You"), I was more than content to bang my head and give those Germans a pair of devil horns while some college flunky tried to score with a high school chick.

The rub to being Jenny Williams's little brother, however, was that people noticed me at a time I might have preferred anonymity. As yet another symptom of the disease became manifest, I had committed to growing my hair long, but the hair itself didn't seem so keen on the idea. My head was Los Alamos, New Mexico, July 16, 1945, a mushroom cloud of strawberry blond expanding outward, down over my ears on the sides; the back was reaching just below my shoulders.

To complicate my appearance, I had gotten braces, which, let's face it, is pretty standard stuff. But Dr. Gandin, my orthodontist, was a creative kind of sadist and installed a special bridge across the roof of my mouth. Every night, I had to insert a small key into that bridge in order to separate my two front teeth slowly, excruciatingly, to make room for all the teeth in my mouth. The result was a considerable gap between my front teeth.

I was a composite sketch of adolescent awkwardness. On the way down to gym one day, I came across a gaggle of football players at the bottom of the stairs discretely passing a joint. They were startled by my footsteps, looking up sinfully until their faces relaxed in recognition.

"No worries," said one of them as he spat a bit of herb from his lip. "It's just *Children of the Corn.*"

I walked past, stunned. This was my nickname in the locker rooms and hallways of Canyon High School? *Children of the Corn*? Their reference to the 1984 film adaptation of the Stephen King story and, more specifically, the character of Malachai, the evil red-headed boy played by Courtney Gains, was in no way a compliment. It could have been worse, I suppose. I could have been the character played by Eric Stoltz in *Mask,* but still, I didn't appreciate the moniker.

Yet to be the vessel of God often requires suffering. So I took my anguish with me from the gym into the back of my sister's Honda CRX, where I squashed into the trunk while her friends smoked Marlboro Lights, sang along to *Appetite*, and talked about whomever it was they were sleeping with that week. I took it all the way up the hill, into our house, upstairs, and into my refuge, the playroom.

There, sometime between getting home from school around 3:00 and masturbating to *Eye on L.A.* at 7:30, The Muse dropped in.

It began, as all rock anthems do, with a riff. Three notes, like "Satisfaction" or "Whole Lotta Love." A C-sharp mixed with a G-sharp? Who had ever heard such a thing? My pinky cleverly slid the G-sharp up to an A. Oh, this was too much. Then the whole thing collapsed onto a B- and F-sharp combo, only to regenerate where I started. I was amazed and infatuated. I could hear all the parts in my head, and I never wanted to stop playing them.

So I didn't.

By this time I had purchased an amp from a pawnshop. It was some ancient pile of crap that had the capacity to annoy my entire block. After I'd played The Riff for the 378th time, my mom quietly knocked on the door and walked in. I stopped, startled, and looked up at her as though in the middle of *Eye on L.A.*

"Honey," she said, cautiously. "That's a really pretty . . . song you're playing."

My amp hummed in the corner, annoyed by the interruption, as if to say, "Yeah, no shit. Who the fuck are you?"

"But . . ." she continued, "some of the guys down in the garage were wondering if you could . . . stop." My father liked a clean garage, so ours was being fitted with cabinets for organizational purposes and the workers apparently didn't appreciate my genius.

She recognized the look on my face and continued. "Or maybe just turn it down?"

Turn it down? Would Mozart "turn it down"? Would Tchaikovsky "turn it down"? Would Nuno Bettencourt, lead guitarist for Extreme, "turn it down"?

I didn't know, either, so I did. But The Muse was with me still. The Riff ran through my head over and over. My art was like the flow of water. You could try to stop it, dam it up, but you could only divert it, causing it to flow in some other direction. So I decided to put down some lyrics to accompany my Riff.

I grabbed a spiral notebook and went to work. I wrote with the fury of a boy possessed. Perhaps I *was* one of the *Children of the Corn*. A Child of the Corn who could smell the early preparations of a mid-week spaghetti dinner. I had to hurry before I was called down to the table, called away from my calling. What if I didn't finish and when I came back after ice cream sundaes The Muse had left, moved on to some other kid down the street?

By the time my mom called, "Honeyyyyy! Dinnerrrrrr!" it was complete. I tossed the notebook in my guitar case and headed downstairs, poetry still flowing through me. I was invincible. Life was going to turn out all right, after all. What did those pothead jocks at school know, anyway? Their team was like zero and eight.

I petted Buck, the family yellow Lab, who congratulated me with a wagging tail and a lick on the face. He knew. Dogs can sense that supernatural stuff.

I took a seat at the dinner table with my dad and sister. As my mom delivered a steaming colander of noodles to the center of the table, I looked at my family with the gravitas of any musical genius, the way you'd see Beethoven looking in one of his portraits, crazy with The Spirit. The lyrics might as well have been tattooed on my face—the music bled from my veins. My family didn't seem to notice and dug into the pasta.

"Sun Angel" was kids' stuff. This was full-grown—ripened on the vine of my torment. This was rock 'n' roll. This was "Living Beyond."

VERSE

Living on the edge
Not knowing where I've been
Living on the streets
And living in sin
Lost from my life
And the rest of my kin
I knew I was gone.

CHORUS

Living beyond all
I saw the light
I have chosen
To give up the fight
Living beyond all
Now that it's gone

All of my life
I was played as the pawn

I suppose we should all be open to the possibility that the gods were breathing through the wrong kid, but the song went on like this for some time. Honestly, a good five or six minutes. It had an adagio, where I talked about voices within and crushing them, followed by a guitar solo with some wicked finger tapping . . . It was an opus for the coming decade, a composition of pure ambition.

As I slurped spaghetti, I wondered: Once I was famous, touring the world with GNR and waking up with lingerie models frozen in the semi-orgasmic poses I had seen in catalogues, would my mom still cook for me?

I brought the song to the group at our new rehearsal space in the garage at Tyler's dad's house. Glen Jacobs's house was a towering wooden structure set back in a small canyon that always smelled of cigarette smoke and dog. The house mascot was Hambone, a basset hound plagued by flashbacks of being abused by a previous owner. If you approached him during one of these episodes, you were greeted by a growl and a clumsy chase that usually ended with either you back in your car or climbing a wall to escape the hound's wrath. I know a basset hound hardly sounds intimidating, but he really was infused with a kind of fury. If you made it past Hambone, you could enter the garage through the side of the house, where we'd set up shop.

Among the old bicycles, lawn mowers, garden hoses, and general clutter, "Living Beyond" was presented to its first audience. Nervously, I tore into the riff, moved through the bridge, nodded to the chorus, wailed through the solo and the refrain, and then pounded the final chord, almost sucking all that sound in from the amp, the garage, indeed, the entire canyon.

I looked around at the faces of the band.

They all nodded.

We rehearsed it, finessed it, and tightened it up. Kyle couldn't seem to get the roll down the toms right. After an hour or so, the Anaheim PD showed up and told us amplified instruments were illegal in the city. We told them no problem, but as soon as they were gone, we were right back on it. Breaking the law.

This was a revolution. We were the youth gone wild, and we weren't going to be suppressed, not by the fuzz, not by any complaining neighbors, and certainly not by the electric shock I got if I touched my back-up microphone and guitar at the same time, a bonus of buying that piece of shit pawn shop amp. After all, this was the will of the gods.

I convinced my parents to buy me a four-track recorder/mixer in order to record "Living Beyond" properly. I could plug each instrument directly into the recorder, then mix it all together like a real producer. We spent hours mic-ing up Kyle's drum kit and then laying my guitar and Sonny's bass track over it. Finally, we added Tyler's vocal track, and we had it on tape.

As we played it back, it seemed fine, but the gods

weren't quite pleased. "Living Beyond" needed an ethereal sense to it, and what we were getting was strictly terrestrial. Too . . . garage-y. With the sun setting and the impending arrival of Tyler's dad returning from work, I needed to think of something quick so we could get this track done and the single into the hallways of Canyon High School.

And that's when the gods seemed to breathe through me. They whispered: "reverb . . ."

Since we didn't have any kind of effects or devices for vocals, I grabbed the four-track mixer in one hand, Tyler's microphone in the other, and told him to follow me. He did, as did Sonny and Kyle, into the house, up the stairs, through his dad's bedroom and into the bathroom, where he had a built-in sauna. Standing in there, I told Tyler to sing, and when he did, the resonance it provided was supernatural, the precise sound the song required. I set the studio up in there, Tyler sang over the music tracks, and we rerecorded it.

As the producer, I put in some clever panning on the second and fourth lines of the chorus, scaled back the drums in certain places, and cranked up the guitar during the solo. By the time Tyler's dad got home with a pizza, we had our masterpiece down on tape, ready for duplication and distribution.

In the hallways and classrooms of Canyon the next day, the reviews were unanimous.

"This is *you* guys?"

Was it a compliment (as in, "I can't believe I get to sit next to you in Mr. Eddy's health class you fabulous/sexy/

talented rock star")? Or was it more of an "I can't believe you losers took the time and energy to make such a piece of crap and then made me listen to it on the only free fifteen minutes of my morning"? We preferred to believe the former.

Suddenly the floodgates were open. The Muse was fused to me, an appendage that kicked me when I tried to sleep and kept me locked in my room while other kids were playing sports, dating, or seeing movies.

On the heels of "Living Beyond" came its companion piece "A World Without Balance." ("When I woke up this morning/And I looked outside/I saw my soul lying to God.") Unclear as to what my soul was doing outside, especially on a school night. ("Cause a world without balance/Is a world without love/We must be together/And learn to live as one.") Before we knew it, we had a nine-song set of entirely original material.

We'd practice every day after school, until Tyler's dad got home and our parents retrieved us. There was, they reminded us, homework to be done. While my rock band was a clever hobby, my parents would tell me, I was in high school now, and my grades counted toward my college application . . . and so on. I'd humor them, of course, but everything else was secondary to The Muse, and chemistry just couldn't hold a Bunsen burner to watching the every move of White Lion lead guitarist Vito Bratta in the "Wait" video.

I abandoned video games and schoolwork in favor of live concert tapes and MTV. Hendrix at Montreal Pop. Ozzy and his lead guitarist, Zack Wylde, in "Don't Blame

Me." Van Halen, Aerosmith's Joe Perry, Steve Stevens and the Atomic Playboys, Eric Johnson, Joe Satriani, Steve Vai, and Yngwie Malmsteen—not to mention the wonderful Ralph Macchio film *Crossroads*.

It wasn't just the music that I studied, either. It was the way these slingers looked: what they wore, their hair, the way they held their guitars, and what kind of straps they used. This was my homework. This was my extracurricular activity. These were my Friday nights.

My parents had much more of a social life than I did. Before they'd go out for FFF (Friday night Fun & Frolic, a monthly staple of the Anaheim Hills Raquet Club), they'd inquire about what I was up to. Wasn't there a football game? After the *Children of the Corn* comment, those guys could eat it. A party? Why didn't I call one of my friends?

Nah, I'd tell them. I was pretty beat. I'd say that I thought I'd just stay in, watch some TV, and cook up some of that prepackaged fettuccine Alfredo. Once they were gone, though, I was in the playroom, guitar plugged in and amp turned up as loud as it would go. My life had meaning.

I called Sonny one evening after I'd figured out the famous climax to the single most important guitar solo ever written, Eddie Van Halen's "Eruption," and I played it for him.

Initially, he didn't believe I was playing it at all, telling me to turn off my stereo. After playing it for him seven or eight times in a row, he finally believed me.

"Craig," he said, barely able to breathe, "if you can play that, we're definitely going to get signed."

This was the single-minded goal of the aspiring rock star: to get signed to a major record label. At fourteen, it became all we spoke of—yet another symptom of our disease. Moreover, with the number of bands being plucked from the local music scene and thrust into the spotlight by MTV, we reasoned that all we had to do to achieve this was book a few shows in the clubs up there, and we'd be next.

By October of 1988, none of us were content to play for an audience comprised of gardening tools and a schizophrenic dog. And the garage was hardly the place to invite people for a demonstration of our talents. We longed for something more. Bright lights. A drum riser. Infinite reverb. Screaming female fans.

We needed a venue.

Shooting You Down

The perception of California has always been fantastic. From Cortés to the miner forty-niners, Hollywood, the Sunset Strip, and the dot-com boom, it's an extravagant (per)version of the American Dream.

The name "California" comes from *Las Sergas de Esplandián,* a novel written in 1510 by the Spaniard Garcí Rodríguez Ordóñez de Montalvo. In it, he describes an island paradise inhabited solely by black women and ruled by the enchanting Queen Calafia, sovereign of the earthly paradise known as California. These women, he wrote, were "robust of body, strong and passionate of heart, and of great valor." Sounds like Ratt's video for "Round and Round," I know.

Naturally, the only metal known to these buxom California girls was gold, which they used to adorn their otherwise naked bodies and collar their animals. Believing they had discovered this mythical island during an expedition in 1533, the conquistadors, led by Hernán Cortés, improperly named the land they found California.

And people's expectations of the place have been over-inflated ever since.

What they actually discovered wasn't an island at all, but a huge deception: the world's longest peninsula that is today Baja California. Dry, rocky, mountainous, and virtually uninhabitable, it's difficult to imagine why the conquistadors thought they had found paradise, except that they profoundly wanted to believe they had.

Even today, the legend of California is perpetuated by some preposterous ideal. Beauty, vivaciousness, an endless springtime, the Oscars, the Rose Parade, and sun-drenched and wide-open boulevards lined with palm trees.

If the rock star fantasy were a state, it would be California.

And like the rock star fantasy, California is best left imagined rather than found. Because the reality of Hollywood Boulevard, where the Oscars are held, is an urban comb-over that is far more depressing than glamorous. And the Rose Parade is dull. And the palm trees lining those car-choked boulevards? They are about as native to the area as the Pennsylvania-born members of Poison.

Yet people continue to flock to the state en masse, only to realize they have been deceived. The brown blanket that stretches from Arrowhead to Avalon isn't smog; it's the collective despondency of millions of people who came seeking California, looking for something they saw on a TV show, or heard in a song, or read about in a 1510 Spanish novel, only to discover the truth.

And the truth is that the mythical island of California doesn't exist. The truth is that this place is made up of a number of smaller, real, nonmythological places. And these places will try to trick you into coming here with epic, legendary-sounding names.

Montebello. Bell Gardens. Temple City.

Or Santa Fe Springs.

Sounds nice, as though there might be virgins in silky white robes frolicking in these springs of Santa Fe, washing their hair in slow motion as if Kip Winger were playing bass behind them. I say the same thing now that the natives must have said to Cortés when the Spanish arrived, looking for busty beautiful black women cloaked in gold:

Don't be an ass.

Santa Fe Springs is an industrial community with 17,500 residents about fifteen miles east of downtown Los Angeles. Factories, refineries, and car dealerships fill the place of the tract housing and strip malls you find in most Southern California communities.

Amidst the smokestacks and power plants of Santa Fe Springs sits a tiny establishment called Chexx. A dark, wooden structure that might host the weekly meeting of the Kiwanis, Chexx offers little to distinguish itself, except that it was here, in October 1988, that Devolution took the stage for its first real, nonplayroom/garage concert.

We'd heard about the place through a band called Venicide, a group of five guys a few years older than us at Canyon High School. The singer, Mike, lived next door to Sonny, and, from my recollection, the band was made up of solid musicians. At the very least, they could play the opening of "Hot For Teacher" and a pretty stellar cover of Credence's "Traveling Band."

Venicide apparently referred to the killing of Venice, but I don't really know how you kill a city, nor do I know what their vendetta was against Venice in particular. Seems like you could pick a more deserving municipality for such violence.

Like Santa Fe Springs.

Venicide often played during the lunch break at our high school, outdoor performances that seemed to annoy the majority of the student body, but I was mesmerized. I'd go back to sixth period and fantasize that *I* could someday perform outside, shirt off, hair blowing back in the breeze, while kids devoured bologna sandwiches, French bread pizza, and chalupas. I'd just have to be sure to wear plenty of sunscreen.

In addition to free rock 'n' roll luncheons, these murderers of Venice had played Chexx a few times, and using them as a reference, we were able to get in touch with Chexx's "concert promoter."

Our determined place of meeting was at the club itself on a foggy school night. Being that we were fourteen, we had to hitch a ride. Being that we lived in Southern California, where serial killers flourish the way Christians seem to everywhere else, hitching a ride was out of the question. Instead, Sonny's father, Kul, volunteered to chauffeur us.

Our limousine for this occasion was Kul's silver Peugeot diesel wagon, which mysteriously always smelled of maple syrup. Somewhere between sputtering onto the 91 at Imperial Highway and getting off at Carmenita, Kul somehow became our first manager. "Let me do all the talking," he told us with a faint Indian accent. "I have negotiated very big contracts."

I don't know what big contracts he was referring to, but Kul's knowledge of the music industry would have been limited to watching MTV with Sonny. Yet Kul loved an opportunity, and he always seemed to have his finger dipped into one extracurricular pie or another: real estate deals, exporting wood to Dubai, or, in this case, managing his teenaged son's rock band. He wasn't a con artist by any means. He was an intelligent man with charisma, ambition, and the connections to make these things work. If nothing less, he was able to convince four fourteen-year-olds that he was the man for the job.

He insisted that he would need printed versions of our lyrics in order to truly help, but I gave him one better and recited "A World Without Balance" for him right there with the rumble of the Peugeot providing my rhythm track. From his reaction, you'd have thought he had just been party to Elliot's first reading of *The Wasteland*. With lyrics like that, he assured us, he could practically guarantee us a record contract. Which, of course, is exactly what we wanted to hear. I know I was sold.

He also had wild ideas about future gigs and began rattling off places we might play in the coming months: the annual fair at the San Antonio Catholic church, the Christmas party at Rockwell International, and even the new retirement home that just opened up on the corner of Canyon Rim and Anaheim Hills Road. All fine and good, we told him, but we wanted to focus first on landing the gig at hand.

We pulled into the Chexx parking lot only to find the place darkened and locked up for the night. Apparently, Chexx was open only on nights when bands were performing, as they didn't have a whole lot of walk-in traffic from the auto salvage yard down the street. The only sign of life came from a rusted out, burgundy Honda Accord, and, emerging from it, like a grub from a partly devoured apple, was our contact.

His name was Ron Nagby and he looked the way his name sounds. Under the orange light of the parking lot, Nagby took us through the photo album he brought with him to show us all the famous people he knew ("See this? Me and Axl Rose. I was there while he was on his fuckin' death bed. . ."). When he finished, Kul got to the point. Four kids, four instruments, longish hair, and plenty of denim—when did Chexx want to showcase the next big thing in the narrative of rock 'n' roll?

And this is where Nagby, in his rapid-fire Philadelphia accent, educated us on one of the finer realities of the fantasy: pay-to-play.

We had to pay a fee up front. Say, $500. Our dividend on said fee was one hundred slips of cheap red construction paper meant to denote tickets. We could sell these tickets at $10.00 each, and, if we sold all of them, well . . .

It was a no-risk proposition for the club. They covered their costs in cash, would probably get a few people drinking overpriced, watered-down booze, and maybe even hawk one of their $5.95 New York steaks advertised on the marquee.

And it wasn't just the Ron Nagbys and Chexx's of the rock world who employed the pay-to-play method. The Roxy, The Troubadour, The Whisky, Gazzarri's— all the legitimate venues did this. Every place we played functioned on a pay-to-play basis, sometimes charging us as much as $2,500 for a night. Because of the deluge of kids descending upon Southern California to take their place among the local pantheon of Van Halen, GNR, Crüe, Ratt, Poison, et al., these promoters could pull it off— without doing any of the actual promoting themselves.

As far as we were concerned, we got a place that didn't house gardening equipment and a basset hound, so we didn't care about the cost. We began to discuss the terms of the agreement with our new manager in the only manner fourteen-year-old kids know.

"Pleeeeease, Kul?"

"We can sell all of them. Promise."

"Sssssseriously, K-k-kul. I kn-nnnnnow we can."

Kul was persuaded and happened to have the money on him, which we then happily handed over.

"Remember," said Nagby, like a wise old captain advising his fourteen-year-old deck hands, "you guys gotta promote the shit outta this show."

And promote the shit outta it, we did.

The next few weeks consisted of rehearsing in the garage, putting the set in order, and occasionally going to school. But classes weren't about learning anything. Classes were about having friends in a confined space, cornering them day after day, and asking, "You bring that ten bucks, dude?" After a few weeks of that, people were paying us just to leave them alone.

Our industriousness is what separated us from other high school kids who start bands, which plenty of them do. I think there were three or four groups at my high school alone (in addition to Venicide, I remember there being an Impaled as well as an Outtlaw), all of whom were pursuing the same metal fantasy as Devolution. Not only did we take the step to go out and book a show, we were diligent in promoting it, dedicating ourselves to the cause with the fervor required of any successful grassroots movement.

At school, we left fliers in the hallway, in the bathroom, and in the parking lot, and we stuffed them into people's lockers.

We had a rebuttal for any excuse thrown our way.

Argument: I don't have the money.

Rebuttal: Come on, dude, your dad's a pilot/engineer/pitcher for the Angels. He makes like two hundred grand a year. He can give you ten bucks.

Argument: My parents don't want to drive me up there.

Rebuttal: There's a van pool leaving from the parking lot of school. We'll get you up there.

Which we did. Using a few vans owned by friends, we were able to guarantee our forced fans safe passage to and from the club.

While we were neglecting our duties as students, Kul seemed to be doing the same with his job as engineer, suddenly taking his duty as manager of Devolution rather seriously. If there's one thing about Kul, it's that he always seems to know someone who knows someone who owes him a favor. Using one of these "connections," he got word to a representative from a record label that a rockin' band of fourteen-year-olds was about to make its debut and that this representative needed to be there for it. And, for reasons known only to this record company representative, he actually agreed to come.

The name of the record label doesn't matter. We'll call it Butt Rock Records. The point was, between our industriousness and our sheer talent, there was no way in hell we wouldn't get signed. We'd have a record contract by Halloween and I'd never have to worry about Mr. Moline's AP English class or *The Elements of Style* ever again.

Indeed, everything was coming together just the way California promised it would.

One of the great clichés of the concert video is the shot where the camera moves down the line of people waiting to get into the club/arena/stadium. Guys with the band's name painted on their chests, girls in white tank tops who flash the camera as it passes by (their breasts always blurred with some frustrating digital witchcraft), and then the band, frizzy-haired soldiers going to battle, seizing the stage with pyrotechnic accoutrement, armed with Spandex-clad leg kicks and twirling drum sticks.

Then there's the Devolution live concert video, and for the great fortune of posterity, it still exists. The cheap, grainy VHS was part of what we got for the $500. However, since it doesn't begin until just moments before the band cuts into "Living Beyond," allow me to take you through a few preshow snapshots from the official Devolution photo album, which also happens to be my mom's photo album.

The first one is of our parents dropping us off two hours before the show for sound check. We had lugged the equipment up in Kul's third and final car, a raised white Toyota 4×4, then dragged our amps and drums through a back door and into the club. Inside the club, little effort had been made to dress up the wooden exterior. Dark, illuminated by Christmas lights, with two pool tables and a stage in the corner, it was like my playroom, except they had a salad bar (with nothing in the way of produce in it) and metal folding chairs lined up rather than a sectional sofa.

The next photo was taken during the sound check itself. There was a thrill not only in hearing the unfathomable amount of echo placed upon Tyler's voice but also in the faceless voice that cracked over the PA, telling us what to do. "Keep strumming your guitar until I tell you to stop." "Now the kick drum." "Need more hi-hat . . ." And so on. This photo shows the man behind this voice, an imp of sorts, thin, pale, with long red hair, at a sound board with his child of maybe three or four in his lap wearing a checkered cape (it was near Halloween). In addition to being the sound check guy, he turned out to also be the bartender, the videographer, and the doorman. Had anyone ordered the steak, I'm sure he would have manned the grill, too.

Then there's the crowd gathered outside the club just before the doors opened. They formed a line that twisted all the way around the building, maybe seventy-five friends, classmates, relatives—anyone whom we knew could spare ten bucks, including . . .

. . . My grandparents?

Sure enough, there they are, looking up at the camera, terrified, although resigned, like POWs. My eighty-year-old grandparents faithfully attended my cousin Jodi's school musicals and cousin Mark's All-American Boy's Chorus performances, so maybe they thought they were seeing some version of *Oklahoma!* Both Lyman and Janice Williams had been aspiring actors in their youths, my grandmother having grown up the daughter of silent film director Paul Powell. My grandfather even appeared in nine feature films, including 1933's *Secrets*, opposite Mary Pickford, and *Dangerous Lives*, a fabulous scare film about syphilis. Upon starting a family, however, they gave up their California fantasy, but they did everything they could to support their grandchildren as they pursued their own. After that night at Chexx, they always looked at me suspiciously, as though I might steal something.

With the crowd seated and the sound checked, I stood stage right. My amplifier hummed as I looked out over the folding metal chairs, now filled by my friends and family. In the back of Chexx, a table had been erected for the record company rep, and behind it was Mr. Butt Rock himself. With seventy-five tickets sold, we had made $250 on the show, which may be the largest profit the band ever turned in a single night. Surely, such business savvy would please Mr. Rock as much as the music itself.

And so, our moment had arrived. With a glorious thumbs-up from sound check guy, our voyage began.

What follows is a transcript of the video that at the time I had imagined would be studied by historians and musicologists alike for centuries.

Devolution:
Live and Kickin' '881

0:00–0:54 ... Only darkness, the sound of our friends and family, eager. A few cries of "Come on, Devolution!" On stage, a figure in white can be seen.

0:55 ... A guitar slowly fades in, and Tyler's voice rings out in the darkness, "Are you guys ready to rock tonight?" Indeed they are, and they let us know it. The opening chords of "Living Beyond" scream into the darkness, the lights explode in an aurora of red, green, and yellow, revealing the figure in white to be Sonny, his dark skin contrasting with his light jeans with holes in the knees, and a white T-shirt with the sleeves cut off. Tyler calls out, "Let me have some drums," and Kyle obliges with the roll down the tom-toms we'd

75

spent so much time on. Slowly, the camera pans over to show Tyler, also in all white, and also without sleeves, a phantasm with his blond hair and pale skin, streaking across the stage. And behind him, Kyle, in black, is engulfed by his double-kick drum set. Finally, the camera pulls far enough back to reveal me, in acid-washed jeans and a black T-shirt, sleeves dutifully removed.

4:30 ... The song continues, our energy fluctuating as we're not sure how to behave on stage. Tyler paces frantically, waving his arms. He calls out, "Mr. Craig Williams," and I step forward and rip into my guitar solo. Finger tapping inspires another roar from the crowd. (This is something to always keep in mind: If you have a big presentation, perhaps a wedding toast, consider finger tapping; people are always impressed.)

5:29 ... "Living Beyond" ends, and there is ... hand-clapping. Tyler asks, "Who's ready to get wild tonight?" There are still a few takers. And so we bust into "I'll Be Gone," an homage/blatant rip-off of Van Halen's first Top 20 hit, "Dance the Night Away."

8:28 ... We move into "Livin' It Up," a rather complex song. It features, as Tyler points out, a bass solo by Mr. Sonny Gupta. Not sure when we received the Mr., but I suppose I liked it. It's how Ozzy always introduced his band.

12:12 ... Sonny breaks into said bass solo, and it sounds like whales gargling. Sonny's bass is an odd quadrangular thing, black, glossy, reflecting the greens and yellows of the stage lights. His hair makes it look as though he's wearing a Darth Vader helmet.

14:33 . . . Sonny hands the bass to Tyler and heads for the keyboard somewhere off camera for the next number. It's called "In the Dark," the second song Tyler and I ever wrote, as evidenced by the song's reliance on keyboard, which Sonny played like the first-chair musician he is. Kyle sits in back, head down to reveal he's wearing a headband, arms raised, sticks twirling à la Poison's Rikki Rocket. I keep my face hidden behind my red mass of hair.

16:54 . . . Sonny goes into some neo-Baroque keyboard solo that can barely be heard over the screams of the crowd. There is a disco ball twirling, poking holes in the darkness.

18:28 . . . Halfway through the set and I tear into "A World Without Balance." I'm banging my head because I believe in what I'm doing and am trying to show what record guy might recognize as "stage presence."

22:30 . . . "Hold on. Hold on a minute," Tyler breathlessly tells the crowd between songs. "I want to do something here. I want to take this time to thank every parent out there who made this possible. Especially Mr. Gupta, our manager." Kul gets his own round of applause, and deservingly so. Tyler then asks if everyone's having a good time so far, and our friends applaud. Galvanized, we launch into a song that, as Tyler points out, is about "a friend of ours who died a while ago. His name was

Jeff, and this song is called 'Why So Soon?'" Musically, the song was something I wrote while trying to figure out "Wait" by White Lion. Lyrically, it really was about the kid who lived across the street from me, who was shot in the head by another classmate with a shotgun. Not gang-land style or anything. It was ruled an accident, but the same kid had the same accident with another classmate a couple years later.

27:06 . . . Tyler announces that it's time for "an all-instrumental song called 'Euthanasia.'" There is the collective question, mostly parents, I think, "Euthanasia?" Where would we learn such a word? Health class. Too bad Mr. Eddie wasn't there to see I'd paid attention. Perhaps he'd buy a ticket to our next show. At Irvine Meadows.

30:39 . . . I think there's a problem with my instrument. I'm sweating—panicking. I think the lights have burnt the back of my neck, but we go into "The Stars at Night." This is a terrible song, meant to sound like White Lion's "Little Fighter," which is itself a terrible song. None of us wanted to do it. We should have filled the space with a cover. But what record company wants to hear "Wild Thing"? Tyler talks to me between verses. "What the hell is wrong with your guitar?" I have no idea. The show must go on. Halfway through, my amp comes back to life. It does little to help.

34:30 . . . With the conclusion of "The Stars at Night," Tyler offers a good night as the crowd roars. But then Tyler wonders in a stilted, rehearsed manner, "Wait a minute . . . You guys want to do one more?" Who, us?

And the crowd cheers, offering suggestions. "Free Bird," of course, but other songs that we don't know. As if we don't know what we're going to play. I hear my sister, "Play 'Sun Angel,' Ty." Only moments later, Tyler says, "Here comes a song called," he pauses here for dramatic purposes, "'Sun Angel,'" and the crowd cheers. They've heard this one before.

36:00 . . . At Tyler's request, the crowd rises to its feet and stands awkwardly, swaying to the song until the last chord fades into the final cheer of the crowd. After just over thirty-nine minutes of exploration, the journey ends, and the video abruptly cuts to black.

We were then allowed an audience, at the table in back where Mr. Butt Rock had been watching, listening, and taking notes. With smiles, hugs, and other congratulations like "Kick-ass show, man," my mates and I took our seats across from Mr. Butt Rock (Record Guy).

Stringy long hair, a bad complexion, sour breath, hairy knuckles, he had a hideous voice that said the following horrible things:

To Kyle: You were off beat the whole time.

To Tyler: You can't. Really. Sing.

To Sonny: I think you need a new keyboard.

To me: Do you . . . like the way your guitar sounds?

And on and on it went. Devolution devastated. However, he liked the "emotion" behind "Why So Soon?"

Kul tried to step in. "These boys all have four-point-oh grade point averages."

We do? Ah, so by "negotiation skills," Kul meant "lying." Clever.

Then Record Guy: "Well, frankly, sir, that doesn't matter. Guns N' Roses didn't even graduate high school."

We would drop out, too, if you'd just give us the chance.

"It does matter," Kul said, his Indian accent suddenly growing more apparent. "These are good boys."

"Really?" Butt Rock scoffed. "Do you know anything about the record business? Who have you worked for?"

There was a pause, and Kul's accent became as thick as the smell in his Peugeot, a cliché.

"I'm in business."

Record Guy just laughed, dismissed Kul and our entire crew, and told us to come back in a few years—then maybe we'd be ready.

Then came that sinking feeling. There was a long, dark, silent drive home, a sleepless night, and an impending flu that kept me in bed the next morning. My mom made me get up anyway.

Then school, which I thought I'd either be skipping or at least pulling up to in some company-owned limousine. Yet, my teachers and classmates knew nothing of the record company exec and the hideous things said. They were just impressed that we had pulled it off.

"My favorite part was . . ."

"That was awesome when . . ."

"How do you do that finger tapping?"

And then class began and all eyes looked forward,

everyone else ready to get back to their normal lives as high school students.

Perhaps I should have joined them—abandoned ship and gone back to being a regular kid. I could keep playing guitar, sure, but I would only bust it out later, in college, while drunk at parties, playing James Taylor songs to impress girls.

But I couldn't. None of us could. The disease is such that it made me, and everyone else in the band, completely incapable of thinking of ourselves as "regular" kids ever again.

We would regroup, take Mr. Butt Rock's advice, reinvent ourselves, and conquer. Given where we'd end up in less than two years, we'd look back on the Chexx show in much the same way a high school freshman looks back on his first day of middle school, amused that his younger self was ever concerned by something so trivial. Where Devolution wrote keyboard-heavy songs that made some attempt at expression, Onyx would trash the keyboard and center everything around effects-heavy guitar. Where Devolution had an amplifier that would cut out in the middle of a set, Onyx would have roadies and guitar techs to ensure that such embarrassments would never happen again. And most importantly, where Devolution would sell a ticket to literally anyone, Onyx would be more discriminate and at the very least be sure to leave my grandparents off the VIP list.

7

Looks That Kill

Devolution, garage days. From left: Kyle, me, Tyler, and Sonny.

It was beginning to appear that the combination of my inspiration, Devolution's collective faith that we would make it, and Kul's connections simply were not enough to guarantee any kind of success. Perhaps a more scientific approach was required in order to discover the best formula for rock godhood.

Fortunately, we had in our midst our own little Dr. Jekyll, Tyler, and his Hyde-like ego to head up our study. Utilizing the scientific method we had all learned in our biology books, we set about conducting our grand experiment.

1. IDENTIFY THE PROBLEM

Devolution continued to meet at Tyler's house, but no music seeped from our garage/laboratory. Instead, we spent our afternoons taking long walks through the canyon that surrounded his house and having extended philosophical chats amongst the eucalyptuses of Anaheim Hills about what had gone wrong that night at Chexx.

I imagine it being not too different from Athens in the days of Socrates, with the notable exception that, rather than dedicated investigations into the development of moral character, we focused primarily on the admission that Devolution's show at Chexx did, indeed, suck, and made inquiries into how we might stop sucking.

2. FORMULATE A HYPOTHESIS

By coming up with an entirely new look, sound, and name, we supposed, our band would be able to live out the rock 'n' roll fantasy that now infested all of our heads. To accomplish such a feat of reinvention, we had several essential tools at our disposal:

- Stryper
- MTV
- Pirate Radio 100.3 FM

 ### Tip for conducting your own experiment at home:

Your tools are an essential part of your experiment and can affect the outcome. Be sure your results are accurate by using calibrated equipment!

Stryper was Orange County's premiere Christian metal group and Tyler's favorite band. Tyler was by no means religious, despite the fact that most of that freshman year he wore white Levi's with a red Stryper "777: To Hell With the Devil" T-shirt. Keep in mind, this is before the days of any Beck/Ween-inspired hipster irony, so it wasn't that either. Tyler genuinely and mysteriously *liked* Stryper's music, even going so far as to modeling his voice after Stryper frontman Michael Sweet. Not only were most of Tyler's early attempts at lyrics blatant rip-offs of Mr. Sweet's, he also employed the same kind of nasal whine that defined Stryper and made them (and, ultimately us) virtually unbearable.

Even more than the sound, however, Tyler was interested in Stryper's look, which consisted of the big-haired, leather-clad appearance that had come to dominate the era. While Stryper wasn't doing anything that the Crüe, Ratt, Cinderella, or a few dozen other bands weren't already doing, they were the first band that Tyler was really into *that dressed like transvestite Vikings*. Tyler's conclusion was that, if we developed a look as Stryper had, it might go a long way in diminishing, or at least concealing, our suck-i-tude.

This look was reinforced by MTV, and in many ways superceded the sound. All you had to do was turn on MTV and see a leather-limbed Kip Winger rolling around with his bass (I don't think he was really playing it) every five minutes to understand this. No one gave a shit what he, or Slaughter, or Firehouse, or just about any other Hair Metal band sounded like; they were just amazing to look at.

Unfortunately, none of us were prepared to drop $400 on a pair of leather pants, and my dad had enough problems with the direction my wardrobe was taking without me strutting around the house like one of the Pointer Sisters. Besides, I didn't even know where one might purchase young men's leather pants. At this point.

Yet, as any able scientist will tell you, necessity is the mother of invention, and a suitable substitute was found in my sister's closet in the form of cotton stretch pants. Young ladies of the late 1980s would wear these pants with long shirts over them to cover the natural phenomenon that resulted, clinically known as "camel toe." On the male frame, we discovered, they cause something a friend of mine referred to as "moose paw," but stretch pants were a way to simulate Kip Winger's appearance without spending Kip Winger cash. Any button-down shirt would work to conceal anatomical issues, although we preferred silk ones with dizzying patterns on them. Paisleys were good, as were polka dots, or any faux animal pattern.

 ### Tip for conducting your own experiment at home:

While Spandex may also seem like a suitable substitute,
even a wannable Glam Metal rocker
will tell you that's really, really lame.

While Tyler, Kyle, and I took to the stretch pants, Sonny handcrafted his own pair of jeans by sewing in gold lamé patches, pieces of black lace, and an American flag over the back pocket. They were tight enough, though, that they still complemented the rest of the band's streamlined look, and he also utilized the silk button-down shirt.

With our look nailed, we moved on to the secondary contributor to our Chexx failure—our music. Tyler argued that songs like "Living Beyond" and "A World Without Balance" were too dark. We didn't want to be Iron Maiden or Queensryche. We wanted to be a fun band—a group that people looked forward to seeing, like the rest of the late '80s Hair Metal bands celebrating America's borrowed economic success. So Tyler took over lyric-writing duties while I held on to the job of writing the music.

No longer did we look to my own torment for source material. After all, I don't know what deep personal angst could have possibly spawned Dangerous Toys's "Teas'n, Pleas'n." Instead, Tyler and I turned to the middle of our FM dial for inspiration: KQLZ, Pirate Radio, 100.3.

If you did not come of age in late 1980's Southern California, I'm sorry for you. Not because you grew up without the benefit of smog alerts where recess would be cancelled for fear that you would die of carbon monoxide poisoning, but because you missed one of the more monumental radio stations ever to grace the dial.

Debuting in the early morning of March 17, 1989, Pirate Radio's gimmick was that some form of pirate, be it brigand or buccaneer, had taken over an abandoned warehouse off Interstate 10 and the signal of what had been an easy listening station. That they played no commercials was appreciated, to be sure, but it was their playlist that made them absolutely legendary.

Nothing. But. Ass. Rock.

It was the perfect station, in the perfect place, at the perfect time. From AC/DC to Enuff Z'Nuff, the music played on Pirate Radio served as a tutorial for what we needed to sound like if we wanted to make it—or so was Tyler's deduction. The Pirate, as it was known, influenced every new song we wrote, and Tyler and I wrote quite a few as our freshman year came to a close.

The most lasting of these tunes would be perhaps our biggest hit, "Another Tear." It was really the result of a jam session in the garage, where I had a chord progression I had taught to Sonny and Kyle, and Tyler simply came in and improvised lyrics over it. The experience was similar to the creation of "Sun Angel," only far more deliberate. "Another Tear" may have been more pop than rock, but the lyrics went like this:

> Another tear is falling
> Although I don't even know your name.
> I know that you're with someone else
> But baby, you gotta give me a try!
>
> Every rainbow has your name.
> Every star in the sky's for you.
> Every time that I pass by you now,
> You just turn away from me.

Your cherry red lips
Your long blonde hair
Every time I see you put that sweet smile
Can't you see the tears from my eyes? Ho!

With our songwriting clearly evolving, as was our look (we could only make our hair grow so fast), the final adjustment in Tyler's experiment was that we needed a new name. Devolution, he contended, made us sound sort of satanic, like Slayer, or Danzig, and that's not what we were going for at all. We needed to convey an image more in line with what was popular at the time. Besides, we needed to distance ourselves from the slapdash amateurs who played Chexx way back in October of '88.

If you could find him, and I'm worried that you might, Tyler would probably tell you that he came up with the new name. Such was the nature of his ego, and he and I would actually argue about it in the dying days of the band. But since I'm writing this book, and since it's the truth, I will tell you that I came up with the name. And it wasn't even so much that I invented it as much as I discovered it—in the middle of my earth sciences book.

Onyx.

When I offered the name to the group for their approval back at the garage/lab, it received a unanimous endorsement. A new band was thus born.

With the new name, songs, and look, the whole thing felt different. Devolution felt like we had been heading backward. Onyx felt polished. By the spring of 1989, we were ready to move on to the next stage in our experiment.

3. MAKE PREDICTIONS

With a newfound confidence (cotton stretch pants will do that for you) came a renewed desire to expose ourselves, once again, in public. We predicted we would play a show at a small venue (probably Chexx once again), be discovered by someone at that show who wanted to book us into other clubs, develop a following, get signed, make an album, get invited to the American Music Awards, date supermodels, and then die tragically.

 ## Tip for conducting your own experiment at home:

Try keeping your expectations within the realm of possibility. It makes science less painful!

4. PERFORM EXPERIMENTS

We contacted our old pal Nagby to set up another show at Chexx, although we did not promote the shit out of our second show as we had our first. We wanted to see if we could actually draw a crowd. We sold a few tickets to close friends, but we were willing to take a loss on this one to see how we'd perform. Luckily Kul was fronting the cash.

Despite the fact that Chexx (and Onyx) attracted an

audience of none, the show itself went swimmingly, and no one can prove otherwise. There was no record company exec there to shoot us down and no surviving VHS tape for a grown-up me to dissect. Phase one of the experiment proved a success.

Yet one successful experiment would hardly garner us the funding of any major record label. By the time our sophomore year started in September of 1989, we decided to try a different venue. With a different "promoter."

His name is Dorian Maye. I can't say, at the age of fifteen, I was well versed in the oeuvre of Oscar Wilde, or bad allusions to Wilde. Of Zakk Wylde, lead guitarist for Ozzy, I could tell you how many hairs he had on each of his nipples. But the fabulous fop of the late Victorian era was a little off my radar. Still, I knew it wasn't likely that Dorian Maye was this guy's real name.

 ### Tip for conducting your own experiment at home:

When handing over $2,000 in cash to some tweaker in skin-tight jeans and a leather jacket, the least you want to know is what name to give the police. Just in case.

I don't remember the name of the club or the city in which it was located. What I do remember is the following:

We met with Dorian at some kind of coffee shop, with Kul still serving as our manager. We gave Dorian a wad of cash, some of which we had scraped together through odd jobs and some of which Kul had loaned us. Dorian gave us 250 scraps of construction paper (green, I think) with the name of his "production company" on them. As in, I'm Making This Up Productions, in association with, Can You Believe How Gullible These Kids Are Media, presents . . . There was a blank space where we were to write in the name of our band.

We sold these tickets to everyone we knew. Anyone we met, we sold a ticket to. People we knew were selling tickets for us. "Hey, I talked to my cousin who lives in Fullerton, and she wants three tickets." She? Here's five.

We even bought a stamp with the name "Onyx" imprinted in a gothic-looking font to stamp onto the tickets because we thought that made them look more legitimate. And we rehearsed, in full costume, incessantly, until the night of the show.

At this time, Kyle's father was in temporary possession of one of those huge Econoline white vans, the kind that only kidnappers and struggling rock stars have any use for. We piled in ourselves and our equipment, and Kul drove us down to the club for sound check.

It was moist out. It was foggy. The streets glistened with an oily mist. The club was in Fullerton, or Garden Grove, or Stanton. There was anticipation in the van on the ride down. Nervous jokes. Secret handshakes. Building to a crescendo of hope and eagerness until we pulled into the parking lot of the club itself.

That's odd. No cars here. Maybe the people who work here live right around the corner and walk. Or take the bus. Because that happens in Orange County. A lot.

We spilled out of the van and headed for the stage door in back. Locked.

We marched around front, tried to pull open the front door. Locked.

We peered through the windows. Empty. Dark.

This is 1989. And unless you are Michael Douglas in *Wall Street,* there are no cell phones. Just a pay phone off the side of the road. We called Dorian Maye.

And he actually answered. We told him that, um, the club appeared to be closed.

Long pause.

"That's weird."

No, Al Yankovic was weird. This was melting my essential organs with mortification.

"I'll look into it."

While there is the chance he is still looking into it, it would seem that we had been duped, as we never heard from Dorian Maye with any sort of explanation as to why the club in which his "production company" had booked us to play was closed that evening.

Then, from that pay phone, we had to call everyone we knew, and everyone we had met, and anyone they knew who had bought tickets, and tell them there was no show.

"Why?"

I think at some point Kyle came up with the idea of telling people there was a gas leak. For the people who did show up, we had cash in hand, ready to refund their money. And later everyone else's.

No one, however, refunded ours.

Tip for conducting your own experiment at home:

Know when to give up!

5. REPEAT STEPS 3 AND 4 UNTIL THERE ARE NO DISCREPANCIES BETWEEN HYPOTHESIS AND EXPERIMENT

This should be the end of this book. Between the first Chexx show and the one that I have just described, we should have been shamed to the point that we simply said enough and moved on. Most people would have, I'm sure. But we didn't. Couldn't. If this experiment proved anything, it's that yet another symptom of the disease is an obliviousness to and tolerance of extreme humiliation. Also, we didn't move on because while we were on the phone letting people know what had happened, Kid Ego was behind the club, kicking its concrete foundation over and over and over again.

Plotting.

8

Something to Believe In

"These guys fucking suck!" said the leather-clad man with a perm in the urinal next to mine. "Bring out Extreme!"

As the rest of the Hollywood cowboys drunkenly endorsed his assertion ("Extreme!" "Yeah!" "Fucking Extreme!"), I zipped up and rejoined Tyler and Kyle in the balcony of Hollywood's Palace Theater, as the band that had so offended my bathroom cohorts fumbled their way through their opening set.

The band was an unknown Seattle grunge act called Alice in Chains. What bothered me wasn't just that I didn't know any of their songs here in the spring of 1990 or that they were so trashed that the singer appeared to be duct-taped to the mic stand while the bassist actually fell into the drum kit. I was bothered because this crap band that would never amount to anything was the last remaining obstacle to me finally getting to see the breathtaking work of Extreme's guitarist/virtuoso/all-around badass Nuno Bettencourt.

Needless to say, the butt rocking community had no idea what was about to hit us. The gritty, depressing sounds emanating from up north were like storm clouds that we all saw, but just assumed, like all storms that roll into the West Coast, would be held north by some invisible force, leaving us to perpetuate the Southern California ideal with our neon pants and teased-out hair.

In addition to Alice in Chains, we had seen Soundgarden play the Whisky, and we thought they were terrible, too. These guys were metal, that much was certain, but where was the sense of fun? Sure, most of them had pretty long hair, but it was stringy, greasy, and could have used some body and texture with a decent conditioner, some Aqua Net, and a blow dryer. And they wore absurd fabrics like flannel, corduroy, and denim. Some of them even wore shorts with thermal underwear underneath! And facial hair? Who were these guys? Hall & Oates?

To listen to them, you'd have thought there was some giant, impending economic collapse or something. "We Die Young," "Man in the Box," and "Sea of Sorrow"? Who wanted to party to that shit? Plus, they had no look, other than to not shower. The music seemed to us simplistic, lacking the instrumental mastery of our heroes, like Mr. Bettencourt, whom I, and many others, considered to be the second coming of Eddie Van Halen. We were like

Glam Metal stockbrokers, and 1990 was our October 1929, rump rock addicts in denial of a serious problem.

In many ways, seeing these grunge bands perform drummed up a kind of faith in Onyx that even Nuno's riffs couldn't arouse, the mantra of the rock wannabe disease: "If these guys can make it," we pontificated, "Onyx totally can, too."

This was something we needed to believe. As a band, we weren't making much headway, to say the least, and as an individual, my grades were slipping, and I was starting to resemble the pale, old version of Bette Davis. And for what? Having some chump rip me off had never been part of my rock 'n' roll fantasy.

As the weeks went on, we needed to move beyond Dorian Maye and our failed science project. Seeing a band like Alice in Chains fail miserably (at least in the short term) was part of the healing process.

But there was also a remarkable resiliency to the four of us, and I think it had everything to do with our age. Youth carries with it less fear about doing stupid things that may cause injury, and should harm be done, the wounds simply heal quicker. Change also seemed to be a natural part of our lives then, which made it seem like there was always hope.

The first change Onyx made was with our management. After all, our latest setback hadn't been a musical one. We never even had the chance to fail musically. This was a business blunder. What, we asked ourselves, would Ozzy, Skid Row, the Crüe, and Bon Jovi have done if Doc McGhee had booked them at the Moscow Music and

Peace Festival and they arrived to a darkened and locked-up stadium? Doc McGhee would be out on his ass.

It was determined then, as a band, that Onyx would dissolve its partnership with Kul Gupta and terminate his services as manager of the band, which I think is how GNR phrased it when they jettisoned their original drummer, Steven Adler. Onyx also decided that since Sonny was Kul's son, he would perform the deed, on his own. Which he did one night, over tikka masala.

Aside from Sonny, no one contemplated this decision more seriously than I. Kul was more like a pal than a friend's father. I just hoped our friendship could survive the dissolution of our business partnership. Fortunately, I think Kul was starting to see managing his son's band as a waste of whatever time he put into it, anyway, so he had no problem with the decision.

To replace Kul, Onyx knew we needed to find someone with music business savvy. Until we did, we all agreed, we would go without management and really work on our end of the bargain, which was perfecting our sound and, more importantly, our look.

Looking like a real rock star, it turned out, was expensive. As I turned sixteen and blew the remainder of my savings on the purchase of my mother's '85 Nissan 200 SX, I set about replenishing my coffers by way of a job in the kitchen of the newly opened KFC–Pizza Hut two-in-one restaurant in the Savvi Ranch business park.

While technically I could be called to duty on either side of the eatery, my job was primarily in the Pizza Hut portion, prepping pies for the day, taking the grease-soaked

dough out of the refrigerator, smothering it with a speci-
fied amount of what management described as "sauce"
and "cheese," and thinking of excuses as to why I couldn't
wear a hair net.

Being the ambitious sort, I also learned the intricacies
of the Colonel's Secret Recipe. Out of fear of a lawsuit by
KFC or their parent company, I won't go into too many
specifics about this experience except to say that I don't
eat at KFC. Ever. But that's a personal choice, and sometimes one must batter poultry in order to rock.

At $5.75 an hour, eighteen to thirty hours a week, I
was able to pocket as much as $150 a week. I disposed of
the money rather efficiently, first into a real amp that
wouldn't electrocute me, a Carvin half-stack with built-in
reverb and distortion. Since no one could ever have
enough distortion on his or her guitar, I also purchased
about a half dozen effects pedals to enhance my ever-
advancing chopsmanship. Then there were back-up mics,
mic stands, home PAs, and a reverb machine for the
garage so that we wouldn't have to record our vocals in
the sauna.

What I didn't spend on musical equipment went into
clothing. With a car, Onyx was set free of the fetters of
suburban mall shopping. My Nissan provided the band
with a direct link to Hollywood, where we'd roll up on
weekend afternoons, wander around until we found the
part of Melrose that doesn't have transvestite hookers on
bus benches, and collectively discuss which mannequin in
which store window looked most like Onyx.

In addition to the dummies were the people walking
around in Hollywood, types we didn't see much—that is

to say, ever—in Orange County. Freaks with teased-out blond hair, makeup to make them appear pale in the California sun, and clothing—magnificent, wondrous clothing.

This went well beyond black leather pants. There was patent leather, blue leather, red leather—colors and patterns I didn't even know cows came in. There were also jeanlike materials, some of which professed bold messages to their audience such as "Fuck."

Then there were the accessories to choose from: vests, head wear (in the wake of Axl Rose, colored bandanas to match one's shirts were a necessity), platform shoes, hobnail boots, ponchos, lace gloves, chaps, cod pieces, masks, belts, bracelets, necklaces, and rings. We were gluttons for Glam Metal style, butt rockin' fashionistas, somehow convinced by the mere absence of this look at our high school that what we were doing was counterculture.

As a purist, there was no substitute for good old black leather pants for me. They had been an essential part of Los Angeles rock godhood since the prehistoric days of Jim Morrison right up to the current Guns N' Roses administration, so I blew about two weeks' worth of saucing and cheesing on my very own pair. Tyler stuck with the cotton stretch pants, choosing to go heavy on the accessories. Sonny stuck with his jeans, and Kyle went for the "Fuck" pants. Footwear for us was a no-brainer. Suede cowboy boots, all black—the defining factors being ornamentation in terms of studs, buckles, and toe and heel guards.

Of course, the more I bought, the more I had to work, and as 1990 ripened, my life became a seemingly endless pattern of hawking pies and rocking out at the garage. Yet, with three of us now driving, the driveway in front of our rehearsal space was growing a little congested. We decided it was time to break out of there and find a real rehearsal studio.

Once again through our rock mentors Venicide, who by now had graduated from Canyon, we learned of a studio called Bands West in downtown Anaheim, nuzzled into one of the corporate parks somewhere between Disneyland and Angel Stadium. It was essentially a warehouse, with storage space for our equipment and perhaps a dozen soundproofed rooms. Each room had its own PA, a drum riser, carpeted floors, and, best of all, mirrored walls so that we could watch ourselves perform and thereby work on our stage presence. Which we did, every day after school, with the devotion of an athlete or a drug addict.

We were also able to garner some outside commentary, primarily from the day manager at Bands West, a Trent Reznor–looking twenty-something named James McFarlane. In addition to collecting the $12.00 an hour we paid for the room, he'd stand just outside our studio, listening. James understood what we were trying to do, he told us, but it wasn't exactly original. He got me to listen to the Cocteau Twins and told me to check out the amount of chorus pedal on their guitar. I did and thought it sounded like angels swimming in honey. Without telling the band where it came from, I started using chorus pedal on our power ballads, and it made them all the more powerful.

"What's that pedal?" they'd ask.

"Oh, it's something Slash uses," I'd lie, and they'd nod. "Cool."

James also had the gall to tell us that Hair Metal was a dying scene and that there were some amazing bands coming up that we should check out, including another local group called Jane's Addiction. Rather than hearing one of the most unique bands of our generation who had, like Soundgarden, one of the best drummers of any generation, we judged Jane's as we would have judged any other band at that time.

"They have no look, James."

"It doesn't matter, Onyx. They're fucking good."

We listened to their demo. "Seven-minute songs? They'll never make it, James. The Pirate won't play it."

Exasperated, James would nod, hand us a mic to use for the afternoon, and direct us to our studio. We'd go through our set, amazed by the way we looked behind our instruments, while James listened just outside the door, less impressed than we, but never tearing us down.

In fact, it was James who encouraged us to book a show on our own. Sure, we were waiting until we found new management to take that step again, but, as James pointed out, no one was going to see us if we didn't play anywhere. By calling the phone number listed at the bottom of an ad for a local club, which read, "For info. and booking info. call . . ." we did book a show, this time at a cavernous venue called The Marquee Club in Westminster, California.

With a capacity of several hundred, a show at the Marquee had every opportunity to be our biggest show yet, but we decided to limit our ticket sales to a select few so as to limit the amount of suffering we would endure in the likelihood the show fell apart. Outside of our families, I didn't think any of us had told anyone about the show, but I'd be proven wrong about that.

My parents had no problem letting me play the Marquee with my friends, as they would have put it. At this point, they saw my rock star fantasy not as an ailment, but as a hobby, perhaps something I could put on my college applications. As long as I was home at a normal hour and sober, they pretty much stayed uninvolved.

With no parents, no managers, no promoters, and no ticket sales, it would be just the four of us—and any rock junkies from the local Westminster area who might descend upon the scene.

When the night of the show arrived, we discovered that the precise number included in that last demographic was somewhere in the vicinity of zero. We should have been disheartened, but we saw it differently: at least the doors were unlocked and the power was on.

The Marquee also had a backstage, which thrilled us endlessly. Not that we really did anything back there, other than hang out and make futile attempts to quell a nosebleed that had erupted from Kyle's face.

In addition to his lingual issues, Kyle had a tragic nasal history. Nosebleeds were for Kyle what drug overdoses were to Mötley Crüe: persistent, inconvenient, but part of life. He was seemingly always visiting the doctor to have his nose cauterized, but the dam would eventually burst, as it did with a vengeance that night, backstage at The Marquee Club.

As we were called to the stage a little after 9:00, all we could do was shake our heads and sigh as Kyle stuffed two Kleenex in each of his nostrils. We were comforted only by the fact that at least no one would be present to witness our latest collapse.

No shirt, "Fuck" pants, blood-stained tissues dangling from his nose, and bare feet, Kyle padded out to the sound of an empty bar, glasses being washed, throats being cleared, and the buzz of neon beer signs. Without hesitating, Kyle did something startling.

He smiled, the gaps between his teeth filling in red, and counted us off, "One, two . . ."

The thing is, we actually had gotten better with all our rehearsing. I don't really remember most of the songs that were in our set that night. There was one called "Jessica," about a girl Tyler met at a mall while passing out fliers for a previous disaster, "Another Tear," and I'm pretty sure we still played "Sun Angel." From watching ourselves in the mirrors of Bands West, Sonny and I had choreographed a few stage moves, rocking back and forth in unison the way Warrant did in the "Down Boys" video, while Tyler seemed preternaturally in command of the stage. He worked the mic stand, and he would then remove the microphone from the stand and pace the stage like a leopard. He put his arm around me during my solos and then would shoot the air with his thumb and forefinger. Being that the place was virtually empty, I don't know for whose benefit this was, but I certainly appreciated the effort.

Between Kyle playing drums with his head tilted back so that he could simply swallow the blood, the vacant venue, and the sound engineer in the back holding up a sign that read "Tune Bass" (because Sonny's instrument was out of tune with mine), despite ourselves, we started laughing.

Behind us, Kyle actually began vomiting back up the blood he had been swallowing all night, and that made us—well, three of us—laugh even harder.

I saw that my big brother had shown up, standing below the stage, tapping his foot and nodding his head, while his girlfriend did a little hip wiggle in time to what we were playing.

I didn't get to see my brother that often. He had moved out of my parents' house and was a drunk. Seemed fitting, I suppose, that he'd show up to see me at a bar, but I was profoundly touched nonetheless. So much so that I dedicated our final song, a torrid cover of Cheap Trick's "Surrender," to him.

My brother loved our version of it, and there was a smattering of applause as we finished, maybe because everyone there was glad we were done or maybe because our "Surrender" really did kick maximum ass. It was applause nonetheless.

As the last chord faded away, Tyler called out his "Thankyougoodnight" for the first time (he must have been working on this in the shower, because it wasn't in rehearsal), while Kyle rushed off the stage to complete his purging.

As we broke down our equipment, the perspiration drying into our silk shirts, my brother came to the front of the stage and hugged me, saying, "Thanks for the song."

I made excuses for the lousy set, which is what any

musician worth his sweat must do after a show. "Kyle, he was, you know, vomiting."

"Vomiting?"

"Yeah. And this guitar, it kinda sucks. I need a new one."

"Shut up," he told me. "You guys did good."

After a few more minutes of awkward conversation ("Where were you Easter?" "You gonna come by for Dad's birthday?" "This is Tracy," he pointed to the woman he was with. "She's pregnant. We're getting married." That sort of thing . . .), he hugged me again and disappeared into the vast darkness of the still-empty club.

In my brother's stead appeared a most unusual sight: two young girls, one perhaps twelve, and the other slightly older, who looked vaguely familiar to me. With them was an older woman, their mom I could only presume. Platinum coif, blinding smile, and, I'll be honest, cleavage like the Sierra Nevada, she looked oddly familiar, too. Not in the same way her daughter did, but just like that woman on the TV show about the radio station in Cincinnati . . .

What the shit was Loni Anderson doing at our show?

They walked right toward us, a *WKRP* trilogy, and when Tyler saw them, he dropped whatever cable he was wrapping, hopped off the stage, and hugged the older daughter. Sonny and I exchanged confused looks (Kyle was still in the bathroom) and crossed over to them.

Tyler introduced us to the older daughter first. "This is Robin . . ." Handshake, handshake, smile, nod. She apparently went to Canyon and was a year behind us.

Then to the younger daughter, "Melissa," yes, yes, fine, good.

Finally to the mother. "And this is Barbi."

Barbi? No, not really.

"Barbara. But everyone calls me Barbi." She hugged each of us warmly. She had heard about our show through her older daughter. Robin worked for the school newspaper, and she had done an article on Tyler and his role for the baseball team. Without our knowledge, Tyler had invited her, her little sister, and her mother to the show.

"You guys were a-*ma*-zing," Barbi told us with a breathy excitement.

Aw shucks. "Could've been better. But Kyle was vomiting."

"Well," still with that crazy wide-eyed smile, "I'd love to hear you guys when he's not, because you sounded great."

"Thanks."

"Do you have representation?"

"No," we said in unison, none more enthusiastic than Sonny. Apparently, a son's allegiance to his father's managerial skills carries only so far.

"You're kidding!"

"No."

"Well, I'd really love to work with you guys."

"Okay . . ."

She handed me her card. It included her photo on the left, her name across the top, her P.O. box number, and her phone number, but the business card provided absolutely no indication as to what she did or really what business her business card meant to promote.

"Give me a call, and we'll talk more about it."

* * *

Barbi lived in a condo with her two daughters near the top of Anaheim Hills. Up to that point, I hadn't really known anyone who lived in a condo. In my mind, condos were where divorcees and singles in their mid-thirties lived, walking around in silk robes and bare feet on their shag carpeting.

Barbi was thirty-eight, divorced from an Italian man named Toreno, which is why her kids had a different last name than her. In addition to her two daughters, she also had a son a few years older than us. The son was some kind of expert trick bicycle performer, hopping around on one wheel, doing handstands on the handlebars, and spinning the front wheel around—that sort of thing. He had performed in the cafetorium of our high school for a talent show at one point and I remember thinking, "Well now there's a skill with little purpose."

Of course, at that time, I had yet to meet his mother.

It wasn't just that Barbi looked like Loni Anderson. Barbi was a student of the actress's life. She was familiar with the entirety of Ms. Anderson's canon, from her first guest spot in 1975 on *S.W.A.T.* as Miss Texas (acting, you see; Ms. Anderson is from Minnesota) to her voicing of Flo in 1989's *All Dogs Go to Heaven.* Barbi knew anecdotes from Loni's childhood and intimate details of her marriage to Burt Reynolds, using it all as a source of inspiration for her own life and passing that wisdom down to her children.

What I don't quite understand is what, precisely, made

her an "impersonator." I remember that, when I was perhaps fourteen, someone hired a Joan Rivers impersonator for my grandfather's birthday. The woman who showed up at my house and interrupted dinner not only looked like Joan Rivers, but also sounded like her and behaved like her—and I couldn't wait for her to leave, which is how I think I would have felt had the real Joan Rivers visited.

I've seen Korean Elvis impersonators who look nothing like Elvis, but sound and act like him, and are therefore successful in their impersonation. Even Marilyn Monroe impersonators can go beyond the white dress and the wind up the skirt bit to sing an orgasmic "Happy Birthday" to JFK, and you get it—you know who they're impersonating.

But I have no idea what defines Loni Anderson, aside from simply being "Loni Anderson." I therefore do not understand how one would "impersonate" her. Or why.

Barbara had VHS tapes of herself on daytime talk shows with other celebrity impersonators during which this interrogative was addressed. Barbi would then launch into a spiel about how Ms. Anderson's life is an inspiration and how she's influenced our culture, trying to sell the woman's celebrity in the same way QVC tries to convince you that Thomas Kincaide is really quite a good artist and therefore you must buy his commemorative plates.

But that's also part of the problem with this particular "impersonation." Barbi wasn't really selling anything. There wasn't any exchange of goods or services by being a Loni Anderson impersonator. She didn't seem to profit, directly, from being a Loni Anderson impersonator. Unless she was doing bachelor parties on the side and I never knew about it.

As a result, she had to supplement her career as impersonator by selling real estate, which is how all people in Southern California supplement their nonexistent careers as quasicelebrities. And with a real estate market that was imploding faster than the local music scene, Barbi undoubtedly needed to supplement that income, too.

I don't know if that's why she wanted to manage a pubescent Glam Metal band. We certainly never made enough money to fulfill that prospect. Maybe she saw us as a way to finally make it into the limelight. Or maybe she just had no sense of rhythm, tone, or melody and truly believed in Onyx and our music. I mean, someone, somewhere, heard something in Mark Slaughter's voice, right?

Whatever the reason, Barbi invited us up to her condo one special afternoon after school. The condo was a split-level townhouse and disarmingly white. The carpet and the walls were white, and there seemed to be nothing but windows with sunlight pouring in. Between the décor, Barbi's hair, and the altitude, there was something quite peaceful about the place.

We all took seats at the kitchen table and, over a pitcher of home-brewed iced tea, Barbi got down to business.

"What is it you guys want for yourselves?"

"To get signed," I answered.

"And how are you going to do that?"

We had no idea.

"You guys are good, but it takes more than that. You need someone to build relations for you—to make connections. You need to refine your look, your sound. I've worked in the entertainment industry. I know how it works."

This all seemed reasonable enough.

"Look at this," she said, crossing to the television and popping a tape into the VCR. "This is a band that just got signed to a huge contract, and they offer a lot of insight into how much work it takes and how it all comes together."

She hit play on the VCR and the band came into view, playing in some dark, packed club with flannel-clad people crowd surfing and generally worshipping at the band's feet. Tyler, Kyle, and I exchanged amazed looks.

"Is that . . ." Tyler started.

"Alice in Chains," I answered for him.

"Good, you've heard of them." Barbi looked back at us, her early '80s bleached blonde coif trying to keep up with the rest of her head as she continued her lecture on the future of the music business.

"What they have is a unique sound and that's how they drew interest."

"Yeah but," Kyle smirked while his mouth tried to catch up to his brain. "But they suck."

"Their contract was the biggest ever for a first-time act."

How was this possible, we mused. Yet again, Alice in Chains made us feel better. If they could land a huge contract, who knows what a band like Onyx could do. We were salivating, and Barbi held the meat.

"You guys need a hook—something that's going to differentiate you from the rest of the bands on The Strip. And what you guys have that no other band out there has . . . is your age. We should emphasize that to draw interest."

That, we all agreed, was a pretty damn good idea.

"You guys," she said, that crazy smile returning to her face, "can be the New Kids on the Block of Hollywood Glam Rock!"

As she passed all of us copies of a contract she wanted us to sign, we were ecstatic, suddenly wide-eyed and smiling just like her. We all raised our glasses in toast, drinking to the possibilities of the '90s with a woman who still looked like 1982, ignoring the future that still played on the VCR behind us, and swilling iced tea as though it were champagne.

Or perhaps Kool-Aid.

Photograph

Onyxx ad from *Screamer* magazine, fall 1990.

According to "Legend 1990," the yearbook recapping my tenure as a sophomore at Canyon High School, much happened over the span of that academic calendar.

The first is that, judging from numerous acts of graffiti throughout "Legend," Onyx appeared to have outgrown the limitations of its four-letteredness sometime that spring and blossomed into the neologism "Onyxx." This was because Barbi had learned of a new band, a group really, already using the name Onyx, and there was some problem with something called "copyright infringement."

The cease and desist papers arrived innocuously enough, in a manila envelope, delivered to the P.O. box Barbi had established for the band for things that she assured us would be coming soon enough: fan mail and requests for tix, demos, and/or official Onyx T's (none of which had actually yet been created). Inside our first piece of post, however, was the most unsettling news. According to a legal team located somewhere in London, the name Onyx was the property of a hip-hop group based out of New York, signed to JMJ Records, the record label run by Jam Master Jay of Run DMC fame.

While DMC's *Raising Hell* was without question one of the most significant albums of the 1980s, and because of its rock-based sound one of my favorites, nothing could have been more off the Onyx radar than hip-hop. By 1990, the genre had become a cornerstone of American culture, with flagship artists like Public Enemy and NWA, but that didn't mean my friends and I had to pay attention to it. Chuck D didn't speak to me, nor was he really trying to, and I wasn't exactly "Straight Outta Compton." Besides, I found much more artistry in Van Halen's "Jamie's Cryin'" than I did in Tone Loc's sample of it in "Wild Thing."

Like metal, hip-hop even had its own show on MTV, which was cleverly titled *Yo! MTV Raps!* In many ways, the genre may have reached its artistic peak by the late '80s, before 1990 brought Vanilla Ice and MC Hammer and hip-hop began its descent into its overproduced phase. Still, Onyx the soon-to-be Glam Metal legends had no idea who hip-hop Onyx were, and in retrospect, it's probably a good thing we didn't.

Hip-hop Onyx were terrifying. They had shaved heads, dressed entirely in black, wore combat boots, and carried knives. While no one knew any of their songs at that point, they were crafting tunes such as "Throw Ya Guns" and "Slam" for the album that would become *Bacdafucup*. It was a long way from "Another Tear," to say the least.

Had we known who they were or their rather unsunny disposition, and given my strict rule of avoiding conflicts with men who carry weapons as part of their "look," we certainly would have acquiesced the name to them. Since we were clueless, much debate ensued up at the condo one afternoon as to whether or not we should change our name. Given the series of humiliations Glam Metal Onyx had endured, we might have just let hip-hop Onyx have it. But Glam Metal Onyx was inextricably bound to that name and so decided to get around any legalities by shrewdly adding another *X*.

Exactly how hip-hop Onyx or their goons in London had heard of the now-legendary Hair Metal Onyx can also be derived from the pages of "Legend 1990." Apparently, Onyxx returned to the stage with a vengeance in the spring of that year, with Barbi aggressively booking shows near the end of the academic calendar and into the scholastic no-man's land that is summer. Our mistake may have been in promoting the shit out of these shows, going so far as to place small ads with our name streaked across in several local rock papers. Clearly, the reaches of attorneys in London know no limits.

Perhaps because nothing catastrophic happened at any of these shows, my recollection of them is, at best, hazy. One cheerleader from my Latin class writes that she enjoyed going to our show and that "you guys are really talented!" How's that for cheerleading?

I distinctly remember this young lady being at the show—up front and rooting us on with the same enthusiasm she would display for our wrestling team. On some level, I'd hoped this cheerleader would see how badass I was away from school and want to have sex with me. She didn't, but I think this reveals an important point about the psychology of the rock star.

Within that crusty leather and hairspray shell lies a gooey insecure center that just wants to be accepted by the pretty girls. This is why so many rock stars date, marry, and then divorce supermodels, the cheerleaders of post–high school society. They are validation for the outcasts. "You may mock my hair and my attire," thinks the rock star, "but you envy my woman." Which then leads to a misogynistic viewpoint, domestic abuse, and, ultimately, songs like the Bulletboys's "Smooth Up in Ya."

Said cheerleader did not attend any subsequent shows, but "Legend 1990" records an almost tactile anticipation for those performances by our real fans.

With Barbi in our corner, we were back to promoting ourselves as though previous humiliations had never occurred. Barbi was at least as desperate for fame as we were, so she really put her heart into getting us out there, enlisting her daughters as promotional lieutenants. Indeed, the Onyxx army was ever growing, as "Legend 1990" also confirms.

By that summer, neither Kyle nor Tyler were members of the Canyon High School student body, having transferred to Esperanza High on the other side of the canyon.

Tyler transferred to flee the wrath of a wrestler whose girlfriend he had slept with, and Kyle left because he was tired of hearing "get a haircut" from other members of the student body.

I'll admit the "get a haircut" comments from teachers and students alike were pervasive, but they never bothered me. To the contrary, I took pride in not being one of the short-haired masses inconspicuously roaming the hallways, listening to Roxette or Bell Biv DeVoe. Like Samson, I found strength in my hair, and any suggestions of cutting it only made me want to grow it longer.

I can't imagine that anyone had it worse in high school than Sonny. Not only did he look like either Milli or Vanilli, but he had always been the butt of jokes simply for being a minority in a community primarily composed of sheltered white kids. To add a thick mop of curly black hair made him not only the focus of ridicule at school, but also within the band. We called him "Dark Helmet."

Tyler and Kyle's transfer to a new school, however, did have the positive effect of increasing our fan base by way of introducing me to my first girlfriend.

Shannon O'Shea was a slight girl of Irish descent, with dark hair and eyes contrasting with pale skin and lightly freckled cheeks. Although merely a freshman, Shannon was much more sophisticated than I. She had dated the lead guitarist of Pretty Boy Floyd.

Pretty Boy Floyd was the next step in the evolution of the Sunset Strip Hair Metal scene, and the band may have been that final genetic permutation that led to the extinction of the entire species. Their first album, *Leather Boyz with Electric Toyz,* featured more hair, makeup, and patent leather than the Crüe, Poison, and Tammy Faye Bakker combined. Despite mind-bogglingly terrible musicianship, vocals, and lyrics (like, "It's Friday night/We're gonna hit the night"), they had become the biggest thing on The Strip simply because of their look, and every rump rock fan worthy of the title anticipated their ascendance to the Glam Metal throne. And although we are still waiting for their ascendancy, at the time, I was oddly thrilled by the fact that this girl had had that kind of contact with one of them.

With Shannon as an obligatory fan, she brought with her several friends from Esperanza. When they amalgamated with Barbi's daughters and their friends, we suddenly had a significant, and supportive, following. Selling tickets for our first show that summer, then, was a breeze.

Rock Around the Clock was an all-ages club in Montclair, California, about an hour east and a decade or so behind Los Angeles. The club itself was in a minimall, right off Interstate 10. You could actually see the sign for the club from the freeway. The outside was rather nondescript: white stucco with a turquoise trim.

Once you got inside, though, the turquoise took over like staphylococcus. There was entirely too much of it and, combined with the neon lights and the black and white tiled floors, the sensation it produced was like being trapped in a Wham! video. It was self-consciously trendy, the architecture for the Ricky Schroeder generation.

The show itself, however, wasn't as bad. Sure, there were some hardcore metal dudes at the bar shouting

"Glam fags!" as we played, but to us this was a contradiction in terms, as evidenced by our almost entirely female audience. Barbi had a mailing list set up by the door, and people actually came up to her afterward.

But Barbi wasn't done there. In order to get our name out with greater effect, no matter how awkward that name itself might have appeared, we had to advertise. And in 1990, there was no other place for a Hair band to advertise than *Screamer* magazine.

Screamer was the bible for the rump rock zealot, a free weekly printed on cheap newspaper that left your fingers covered in ink. It printed concert reviews of local acts and articles about the scene, but the main attraction was the ads, and there were pages and pages of them.

Each ad used the same template. First, the photo of the band in an absurdly unnatural pose. This pose could be erotic, it could be disinterested, or it could be vicious. Not vicious in an "I'm going to eat your face" manner, but vicious in an "I need a home and a shower and some soup" way. Hair was teased and clothing was sadomasochistic. Across the bottom of the photo, but in no way obscuring it, would be the name of the band. Tuff. Friction Addiction. Badger. Lush. Tryx. Paradise. Pair-A-Dice. Baron Von Rock. Freak. Swingin' Thing. Onyxx. And on and on for dozens of pages. The bigger bands took out full-page ads, which ran for two grand or so. From this advertising pinnacle, rates ran all the way down to tiny announcements in the corner for seventy-five bucks.

Most of the ads promoted upcoming shows or heralded which college radio stations the band had been played on. Some of the bands were just there to be seen, ads for advertising's sake, or to attract a record label. Without fail, however, the centerpiece of any of these ads was the photo.

Onyx and, yes, even Onyxx had placed small ads simply with the name of the band and a show date. What we were missing, Barbi pointed out, was a professional photograph so that we, too, could have an ad that would match the ass rock template. Naturally, she had a photographer who had done her head shots, so she set up a time for Onyxx to drive up to Hollywood and take part in our first professional photo shoot.

The day of the shoot, I spent the morning blowdrying my hair to the point of perfection, so that it cascaded from my scalp like a waterfall in an Ansel Adams photograph. It also took me some time to pick out the perfect shirt, which turned out to be a simple black silk buttondown. The leather pants were an obvious choice, although there was a brief moment of panic when I couldn't find them in their usual spot folded on the top shelf of my closet.

"Mom," I called downstairs, "have you seen my leather pants?"

"They're in your closet, on a hanger, where they *belong*."

Sure enough, they were, although I'd have to talk to my mom about going through my closet a few months later when she found my funnel attached to a plastic hose next to my baggie of "oregano."

I grabbed my sunglasses and paced, waiting for Barbi to arrive, as she'd volunteered to carpool all of us up there.

When I saw her car pull into the driveway from my

bedroom window, I bound downstairs just in time to see my mother open the front door. It suddenly occurred to me that my mother had never met my manager before. Don't know if Emily Post has protocol for that one.

"Hiiiiiii," they both said in faux excitement. "It's so nice to meet you."

The way they spoke in unison disturbed me.

"Carolyn," Barbi said, "I just want you to know that I think Craig is a terrific kid."

"Yes, he is."

I think we could all agree on that.

Barbi continued. "I really feel like a mother to these boys." My mother took a step back, her smile tightening into more of a teeth clenching. "If you ever need any help raising Craig, I just want you to know you can give me a call anytime."

"Oh," my mom said, her jaw muscles bulging through her cheeks. "Okay."

While I believe Barbi probably meant well, this just wasn't the sort of thing you said to my mother. Why would she need help raising me? Was she incapable of doing so on her own?

"Well," my mom said, "I'll let you guys get going. It was *so nice* meeting you."

They both agreed and, with that, my new mother-by-proxy and I were on the road.

We met the photographer on a street somewhere in Hollywood. I was really too young to make sense of the geography of the City of Angels then, but it seems to me now that it may have been Beechwood Canyon, a street of grand old houses converted into apartment buildings that, as you're heading up it toward the hills, perfectly frames the Hollywood sign.

The photographer was waiting for us, leaning on the hood of a beat-up Datsun and wearing tight black Levis and an old leather jacket. He was gaunt, a bit weathered, but nice enough, with various pieces of photographic equipment dangling from his shoulders.

Our posse roamed the neighborhood for hours, finding different spots to stop, pose, and snap a roll or two of film. Passersby would stop to stare at the celebrities we all imagined we were, Barbi fielding any inquiries.

Finally, we found a secluded alley behind an apartment building, and the photographer positioned us in a back doorway. He told Kyle to get up on the top step and positioned two stools for Sonny and Tyler to sit on in front of our drummer. I climbed in behind them and threw on my sunglasses. He told Tyler to put his hat on and Kyle to tilt his head just a bit, a little more, a little more, right there . . .

POOF!

The rails of a fire escape provide the photo with a rakish frame, matching perfectly with the tilt of Kyle's head. Kyle is the only one smiling, staking his claim as the playful one of the group, while the rest of us look either angry or medicated. I am leaning over just next to Kyle, my hand on Tyler's right shoulder, my leather pants obscured by Tyler's torso. Next to Tyler sits Sonny, shirt unbuttoned to his navel and a giant hoop earring in his left ear. His arm is draped over Kyle's leg, notable for the fact that Kyle's ripped white jeans barely obscure his "fuck" pants. Behind us is a trashcan and a concrete wall, a gritty, urban backdrop, a carefully crafted image of reck-lessness.

Once the photo was snapped, Barbi embraced us, told us, "That's the one," a proud mother whose babies just had their first portrait taken.

Within weeks, that photo would appear for the first time in the pages of *Screamer,* a quarter-page ad that cost $250 announcing several shows Barbi had booked for us later that summer.

This photo would be silk-screened onto T-shirts and photocopied onto fliers. Later, autographed glossies of it would be framed and hung in clubs where we performed or mailed out to members of our fan club.

And thus, the real legend began.

10

Once Bitten . . .

There are landmark moments in every young person's physical and emotional growth that forever alter that person, as any study of human development will confirm. We roll over; we crawl. We take our first steps, we speak our first words, and, eventually, we are trained in matters of the potty.

Then, for a long time, nothing happens as we attempt to perfect these basic skills—until approximately the sixteenth year, when we all come to the same life-altering realization: "Holy fucking shit!" we inevitably say to ourselves, musing just as the intellectuals of antiquity would have. "I have groupies!?!"

For some, that moment comes after a three-night stint

at the Greek Theater. For others, it comes after a sold-out engagement at Madison Square Garden. For me, for Onyxx, that realization came about halfway through our set on a hot summer night in 1990 at a place called The Palomino Club in North Hollywood.

While I won't go so far as to say that girls were the sole reason we'd formed a band, they'd certainly always been a part of the fantasy, since the days Devolution rocked the playroom of my parents' house. There are fundamental differences, however, between being lucky enough to have girls come to your gigs and having groupies.

Girls come to your show because they know you and want to support their friends. Groupies come to your show because they've heard of you. Perhaps they've seen a photo of you in a certain weekly publication that's circulated around town, and they want to get to know you.

Girls are your friends and can therefore offer you genuine criticism, from individual songs to set lists to wardrobe choices. Groupies are unflinchingly supportive, and no matter what you do, they wiggle their hips, throw their bangled arms in the air, and squeal "Yeah!" or "Woo!" They uses phrases like "right on" and "sweet" regardless of context, so that the groupie opinion is inconsequential.

Girls come over to your house on summer afternoons to swim and barbecue while your mom brings you iced tea from inside and your older brother watches ominously from the darkened confines of the bedroom he's been occupying since he had his driver's license revoked for driving while intoxicated. Groupies come back to your room at the Travelodge to see what kinds of drugs and booze you have and perform sexual favors for you in a closet or a shower while your manager delivers more of whatever it is you need.

The difference between having girls come to your show and having groupies is the difference between being in a band and being a rock star.

Up until the summer of 1990, the regulars at Onyxx shows had been friends of ours, primarily my girlfriend Shannon and her friends. In addition to being the first girl I made feeble, momentary love to, Shannon was also the first person outside of my family to tell me that she loved me.

This was earlier that same summer, standing in the doorway of her parents' house after a heavy meal of Mexican food, which is what precedes most romantic occasions in Southern California. I was keenly aware that this was a seminal moment in my life and wanted to reciprocate by telling her something romantic, something she would remember for the rest of her life, but also something only I could tell her.

"You know," I whispered softly, my lips close to her ear, "I sometimes think about you when I'm, you know, playing one of my guitar solos."

There was a long silence as, I was sure, she was swept away with emotion, holding back tears. She pulled away from me a little, looked into my face, and cocked her head ever so slightly to the side.

"You mean, like, I inspired the guitar solo?"

That which is open to scrutiny is threatened with meaninglessness.

"Not exactly, no. Just . . ." How could I explain this? Why did I have to? "When I'm playing . . . I'll sometimes . . . I think about you."

"Oh." There was another long pause. "So did you write the solo about me?"

I didn't know what I'd meant by it; it just seemed like a unique response. Now I wished I hadn't brought it up in the first place, so I just muttered, "Yes."

She nodded. "Cool."

Then we made out.

When I wasn't romancing Shannon out of her miniskirts, we were hanging out with the rest of the band and Shannon's friends. Most days were spent listening to The Pirate, talking about which bands Onyxx was better than (Trixter, Slaughter, Gorky Park, Steelheart, among others; we weren't really better, of course, but this was another symptom of the fantasy . . .), and sucking down cigarettes in the driveway of Shannon's friend Chrissie's house.

Chrissie was hopelessly devoted to Tyler, convinced that Tyler had written the lyrics for "Another Tear" specifically for her. While there was the lyric "Your cherry red lips/Your long blond hair," and Chrissie happened to have those requisite features, the song was intentionally vague, precisely the sort of thing that could cause a variety of girls in the audience to think, "He's singing that about *me*!" Psychological manipulation is yet another reason sociopaths make the best frontmen.

As far as Tyler was concerned, Chrissie's devotion gave

him license to torture her. When her parents weren't around, and I don't remember ever meeting them, she'd parade around in a g-string, flash her breasts, and then hop in Tyler's lap and try to lick his esophagus.

The more Tyler denied her, though, the more fervent her attempts became. At one point, she threatened to leap from her bedroom window if she couldn't have him. Tyler laughed and told her to jump, which wasn't as cold-hearted as it sounds since her window was perhaps eight feet off the driveway. We figured at worst she'd sprain an ankle.

Allison was the funny girl of the group and had a thing for Russo, one of our friends who over the course of the summer began to act more and more as our roadie. Since Allison was a nice girl, she looked right past Kyle and his predictable requests for blow jobs (a staple of Kyle's since the Camp Snoopy incident) and focused her affections on Russo.

Finally, there was Sandy, a pale, thin girl with a thick head of curly red hair who wasn't interested in any of us. She was simply a music fan, decades more mature than the rest of us and, perhaps more than anyone, the critic whose opinion I valued most as far as our songs went (such as which ones we should work on replacing).

These girls were always the first to buy tickets to our shows, and on the night of the show at the Palomino, they were the only ones who had bought tickets. This was not the fault of our management, as Barbi had booked the gig with the knowledge that a show in the middle of summer break would be difficult to sell. Many kids were on vacation with their parents, but it was also the season of the stadium show, when bands much bigger than Onyxx were out on tour, playing venues much bigger than the Palomino in North Hollywood.

Yet it was the fact that a certain band was away on tour, in conjunction with our latest ad in *Screamer*, that gave birth to a milestone in Onyxx's development.

The Palomino is a tiny space on Lankershim Boulevard, not far from Universal Studios. While it wasn't quite The Strip, it was certainly one step closer than Chexx. The stage was barely big enough for the four of us, particularly with Kyle's oversized drum kit, but the show had been going well, our girls at the front of the stage singing along to all of our songs, and applauding and screaming between them.

What I remember then is white. The skirt, the heels, the tank top, but especially the hair, cosmic in its size and intensity. Her skin was dark summer brown so that, with the white mane atop her head, she sort of resembled . . . well . . . a palomino. My first instinct, actually, was that she, and the four or five twenty-somethings just like her who followed, worked for the club somehow.

We were in the middle of a song, so we could hardly discuss the matter among ourselves, but our girls certainly were. Before they could reach any kind of verdict, however, they were literally pushed away from their designated spots at the front of the stage and deposed by the new ladies.

These new ladies looked up at us, smiling, dancing, and clapping their manicured hands while our girls looked on in awe. As the song reached its climax, Tyler leaned down and sang directly to the head palomino, who pretended to swoon, winking and smiling at our frontman.

We went into the next song, a power ballad, the name of which escapes me now, but I know I had a cool backing vocal where I got to scream, "And I can't stand the pain!" We weren't twenty seconds into it when, as if on cue, each of these ladies pulled out twelve-inch white candles, lit them, and held them over their heads, swaying back and forth to the song. The lighting person at the club dimmed the lights so that all we could see were the ladies lit by the candles, our girls and everyone else fading into shadow. This only furthered my suspicions that these ladies must have been in the employ of The Palomino Club—or perhaps the city of North Hollywood itself.

Imagine my surprise, then, to discover at the end of the night that they weren't really on anyone's payroll. As Russo and another friend broke down our gear, these ladies approached us with the information that they'd seen our ad in *Screamer*, thought we looked hot, and had come down to see the show. Ah, the power of positive advertising.

The head palomino, who had one of those names that you usually hear only in movies that appear on premium cable late at night, like Mia or Tara or Kyla, did most of the talking while she clung to Tyler. "You guys wanna come back to our hotel room and party?"

There would never be such a unanimous band decision again.

I had never partied before. I'd been to parties. I'd even been to a hotel room. But I'd never partied in a hotel room. I had no idea what went on in such an environment.

What I did know is that I had a girlfriend, she loved me, and I thought about her when I soloed. I asked if I could bring her and her friends with us.

The ladies looked at our girls, who suddenly looked like shaved cats shivering in the corner, and smiled. "Of courrrrrse."

Once Shannon and her friends crammed into my car, I followed the rest of the crew to the hotel, although I can't say Shannon was particularly excited about heading over there. I had to, I told her. This was a new fan base. I needed to be cool to them. I didn't want to, of course, but, shit, what could I do?

By the time we got there, the party was in full swing. There was champagne, beer, a little weed, carts of food from room service. The head palomino was in Tyler's lap as they passed a bottle back and forth. Even Shannon and her friends lightened up a little when they saw the spread.

What we came to find out was that these ladies were Beverly Hills girls, the daughters of dentists and surgeons, who spent their parents' money indiscriminately. They were veterans of the music scene and normally spent their nights in much the same manner as they were spending this night with us, but with another band.

That other band, they told us, had just left on tour, so they were looking for some other guys to party with for the summer. Onyxx had won the lottery.

"Whhhhhhho do you g-g-g," Kyle took a swig from a bottle of Grand Marnier, his arm around the waist of a denim-skirted one. "Who do you guys normally hhhh-hang with?"

"Have you heard of Great White?"

Had we heard of Great White? I loathed Great White! They were long-time veterans of The Strip who hit it huge with their version of the Mott the Hoople song "Once Bitten, Twice Shy." Really, I had always been baffled as to how what was essentially a cover band had come to such prominence. That summer, Great White was co-headlining a tour with Tesla.

It suddenly hit me as I looked out the hotel room window, the lights of the San Fernando Valley spreading out infinitely like a promise. Here we were. Partying. After a gig. In a hotel room in the valley. With Great White's groupies! And they wanted to be our groupies now!

There had never been any doubt in my mind as to how I wanted to spend the rest of my life, but right then it seemed that it might actually happen.

I can tell you the exact moment the emerging "Alternative" music scene finally made sense to me.

It was that same summer, at Tyler's dad's house late one night (or very early in the morning), and there was a woman of perhaps twenty-two removing her clothing piece by piece in Tyler's dad's living room to the cassette single of Jane's Addiction's "Mountain Song." (Tyler's dad, needless to say, was out of town.)

As she swept past me, naked as a bar of soap, fire roaring in the fireplace behind her, I thought to myself, "This song's pretty good."

Although a stripper by trade, the woman was by no

means on the clock at this exact moment. She was a friend of Tyler's, someone he'd met at one of the gentlemen's clubs he'd (okay, we'd . . .) been frequenting that summer.

We still needed our fix, and as thrilling as the prospect of starting junior year was, the girls at our high schools would hardly work as stand-ins.

There was also the minor problem that the girls at our high schools wanted nothing to do with us or, more specifically, me. Sure, we were huge in North Hollywood, but in Anaheim Hills, I was just some awkward long-haired kid.

The question, then, as I approached my junior year, was not when I was going to take my SATs or where I was going to apply to college, but where I was going to find more women in their twenties to feed me, get me drunk and high, and come to my shows and tell me I'm wonderful. As with everything else in my life at that time, I turned to MTV and The Pirate for guidance.

With references to Hollywood's myriad strip clubs pounded into our brains by songs and videos like the Crüe's "Girls, Girls, Girls," which was apparently about girls, or "Every Rose Has Its Thorn," which Bret Michaels wrote about a stripper who broke his heart, we figured hitting up some strip clubs was appropriate. I mean, if rock stars do it, it has to be okay.

Problem was, at sixteen, there wasn't a strip club outside of Tijuana that would let us in. Somehow, and I never really got all the details on this, Tyler found a check-cashing store in Santa Ana (the "gritty" part of Orange County) that issued IDs. For $10.00, we got a cheap, laminated card with a small photo in the corner, which, to guys used to doling out hundreds of dollars for pieces of construction paper tickets, seemed like a pretty good deal.

The ID included date of birth without actually asking for proof. Suddenly, we were eighteen, at least in the eyes of Julian's Check Cashing. Using it at actual strip clubs, however, would be another story altogether.

For our first attempt, we dressed in our stage clothing—boots, pants, and all—because we thought this made us look grown up, or at least like the rock stars we'd seen on television. We drove up to Sunset, starting at The Seventh Veil, one of the clubs referenced by Vince Neil in "Girls, Girls, Girls."

With the rush of traffic on Sunset behind us and the muted thump of music coming from within the club, we strutted up to the door, only to be stopped by a mutant bouncer who seemed to have legs for arms.

Seventh Veil bouncer: "Can I see some ID?"

Me: "No problem." Hand shaking as I reach into back pocket of leather pants, undo Velcro wallet, and hand him check-cashing ID. "Packed in there tonight?" Gulp. "Bro?"

Seventh Veil bouncer's eyebrows furrow as he looks at check-cashing ID: "You gotta fucking be kidding me, kid."

Some kids might be deterred by this and just head home. But we were Onyxx. We walked back to Tyler's El Camino and slowly headed east on Sunset . . .

. . . To the Crazy Horse on La Brea . . .

Crazy Horse bouncer: "Kid must be fucking kidding."

. . . To Jumbo's Clown Room . . .

Bouncer cackles like an evil clown: "Fuck off, kid."

. . . And farther east, and farther east, and farther east, rejected at every stop, until we found ourselves halfway to Las Vegas. In Ontario, to be precise, the capital of Southern California's Inland Empire.

In addition to being renowned for its meth labs, Ontario has its own international airport. More importantly, it has a Déjà Vu outpost, the chain of strip clubs with locations nationwide. More important still, it seems the closer one gets to Vegas, the fewer laws that are enforced.

This time, we came up with the idea of approaching the door with cigarettes in hand, adult garnish to complement our IDs. After all, you had to be eighteen to buy smokes, right? We handed our check-cashing IDs to the bouncer, who looked them over, looked at us, shrugged, and waved us in.

Tyler took the lead and I followed him inside. As he parted the velvet curtain that led into the main room, we stepped in and were engulfed by music, body mist, and light.

While there are many names for stripping, from the legitimizing *dancing* to the more common term *adult entertainment,* to H. L. Mencken's euphemism *ecdysiast,* very little is known about the history of the strip club itself.

The striptease has roots back to the Sumerians where,

it is written, the goddess Innana descended into Hades in order to rescue her lover. During her journey, she passed through seven gates, removing an article of clothing and a jewel at each one as her toll. This dance was replicated in the Bible by Salome during the dance of the seven veils (and gave birth to the name of the club on Sunset, no doubt), and thus a culture of crumpled dollar bills, weak drinks, and high-fiving was born.

By the late nineteenth century, Europeans brought a version of the striptease to Paris in the form of burlesque, wherein the intent of the whole thing was veiled as "a woman removing clothing in a vain search for a flea."

After WWII, stripping was at last Americanized, packaged, and of course stigmatized, where it then spread across the United States along with prefab housing, shedding any pretense over the decades as to its purpose. Until the summer of 1990, in Ontario, California, by which time stripping had simply become a group of women simulating friendliness and interest in men in order to bilk them out of money.

I slid into a booth with Tyler and ordered up a soda and stared slack-jawed at the topless woman hanging upside down, her legs twisted tightly around a copper pole. Other seminude women walked past us, smiling, while in various corners, men received lap dances.

"Dude," I said, leaning over to Tyler. "We should come here more often."

We did. Pretty much every weekend. At first, it may have been a little awkward as we constantly turned down offers for lap dances. Not because we were above it, but because we didn't actually have any money. Eventually though, as we came in more often, the talk drifted away from prospective dry humping and grew more personal.

The question was never if we were in a band, but what band were we in. Soon, invitations to our shows were extended; we may not have had any money, but we certainly had tickets. "August 2nd, Rock Around the Clock in Montclair. You should totally come." Some of them did, and sooner or later friendships were formed.

We weren't exclusive to the Déjà Vu in Ontario, of course. As much as we enjoyed the drive out there, we continued our search for other venues that would accept our check-cashing IDs. After some amount of wandering, we stumbled upon a place on Hollywood Boulevard called The Cave, although I don't think the man in the glass booth even checked our IDs at The Cave. As long as we could pay the $3 cover and weren't armed, we were in.

The Cave housed an adult bookstore in front with men in heavy coats browsing through the titles. There were quarter-operated video booths, and a door led into the back, The Cave itself.

It was a cramped space with a small stage lit by Christmas lights and filled with cigarette smoke, not from the patrons but from the dancers. I think some of them actually smoked while on stage. The place was cold, even their Sprite tasted rank, and no one ever seemed to be there, which had the advantage of forcing the women to talk to us.

It was here that we befriended the group of ladies led by Baby. She was a considerable brunette woman in her twenties who not only stripped, but was also involved in the world of phone sex. For whatever reason, she took to me with a protective kind of affection and would call me at hours of the morning that displeased my father.

"Listen," he told me one sleepy weekend morning, "I don't know who 'Baby' is, but can you tell her not to call after ten?"

Baby thought it was cute that I lived with my parents (where did most sixteen-year-olds live?), and when I told her my father's request, she gave me her phone number instead.

I called frequently.

It became apparent that we had descended into something like Hades, however, when we met Baby's best friend, and fellow ecdysiast at The Cave, Frenchie. She was, not surprisingly, French. What was surprising was that she was working the pole while pregnant. Clearly not the sort of thing one saw in any of the Crüe videos.

In addition to attracting groupies and validating us in the eyes of strippers, the Onyxx ad that had been placed earlier that summer in *Screamer* is also what attracted the attention of *Sunset Strip Magazine* Band of the Year Swingin' Thing and their charismatic frontman, Paul Bardot.

Mr. Bardot invited Onyxx to open for Swingin' Thing at a show at Rock Around the Clock on August 23. Between us in the supporting slot would be another quickly rising band on The Strip, Baron Von Rock.

BVR, as they were known, was composed of only two members, Mikey and Markey, one on guitar and the other on drums. They used a prerecorded bass track for their Ramones-inspired pop/punk/Glam Metal blend and wore tight jeans, Chuck Taylors, and neon pink hats backward, with their black hair hanging over their faces. They were, along with Swingin' Thing, among my favorite bands on The Strip.

What was remarkable was the reverence with which we held these stars of the Sunset Strip. It didn't matter that no one else had ever heard of them; we had, and we believed everyone else would soon enough. For us, we might as well have booked a gig with Poison.

Yet playing with Swingin' Thing and BVR also made sense. It was a realistic opportunity for us. If it worked out, we would book a show with those guys on The Strip, get signed, and maybe even skip our quickly approaching junior year.

We also managed to find time to party just about every weekend with our groupies if they were available, and if they weren't, then we'd party with any strippers we could find. Sometimes the groupies would have a hotel room or, if Tyler's dad was out of town, they'd come down to us. These ladies didn't replace Shannon or her friends, but I can't say Shannon was always around, either.

Nor would she be for much longer. Shannon, my first love and number one fan, was moving away. Her father was retiring to a community in eastern San Diego called Fallbrook, where people were quite fond of the avocado. Although the move would happen in time for her to start school down there that fall, it would not be before our show with Swingin' Thing on the 23rd.

I'm not entirely sure I believe in defining moments as much as I believe that there is the culmination of a series of events when you suddenly realize things are different. One night, promoters are cheating you out of money and the clubs you're booked into aren't even open, the next you have 250 groupies packed into an obscure venue in an obscure city clamoring to talk to you and they're offering up their mammary glands for inscription.

Such was the occasion that August 23, 1990, at Rock Around the Clock.

Nothing changed in me, personally. Perhaps because I wasn't involved in every detail of our band's sudden rise to fame, I couldn't see the evolution of each of these moments and could see only the end result.

And I'm not talking about the miracle of ink flowing across tender untouched flesh. I'm talking about the heat of hundreds of eyes upon you. I'm talking about looking out and seeing people you don't really know mouthing the words to a song you wrote. I'm talking about the sound it makes when those same people sing aloud to one of those songs, usually a power ballad. I'm talking about four wannabes who suddenly, and inexplicably, were.

If there had ever been a time when I might have been healed of my affliction, this evening killed any hope of it. The fantasy that had begun in my head had metastasized, taken over my entire body, and I was hopelessly, irrevocably lost.

When the show was over, Barbi found each of us in different corners of the club. We were surrounded by well-wishers, autographing pieces of paper and body parts alike. She pulled us all together, breathless.

"You guys were amazing," she told us, shaking her head. "This changes everything. An A&R rep from Capitol Records is here and he was blown away."

Artist and Repertoire representatives were the people who combed the streets looking for new talent to sign to record labels. He had come to see Swingin' Thing, she said, but he was now interested in Onyxx. Barbi was taking off to have drinks with him and talk about a possible record deal.

This was how it happened, I thought. Unexpectedly, suddenly, overnight. We all went back to our respective homes and lay awake in a dream, waiting for Barbi to call and tell us how much money Capitol Records wanted to give us to record our music.

But when the phone rang later the next afternoon, the answer was none. Capitol wasn't interested in another Hair band, even if we were just sixteen, because they had just signed a Strip band called Cry Wolf. It was gut-wrenching news, but Barbi was optimistic.

Because of the profile of Swingin' Thing as the next big thing, dozens of other promoters and managers had come to the show and, having seen the reaction of the crowd, all of them wanted to book us. If nothing less, these music industry types knew we could fill a place with people.

Which is why we placed another ad in *Screamer*, adding several shows:

Sat. Oct. 6—Spanky's Riverside
Thurs. Oct. 11—Rock Around the Clock
Sat. Oct. 13—The Roxy
Thurs. Nov. 8—The Troubadour

Indeed, within weeks, we would make our debut on the famed Sunset Strip. It was only a matter of time, Barbi assured us, before we had more A&R reps at our shows and were signed to a record contract.

As the summer came to an end and I helped Shannon's family load boxes and furniture into a moving van, I made the pointed overture of buying her a cubic zirconium ring as a symbol of my promise to make the ninety-minute drive down Interstate 15 to visit her. But by then, too much had happened. I had been bitten, more than once, by the allure of photo shoots, groupies, strippers, record label A&R reps, and breast inscription. I realized that *no* relationship could withstand the temptations of the rock 'n' roll fantasy, which I think is what the Crüe was trying to tell me in "Home Sweet Home."

Kissing Shannon's tear-swollen lips for the last time while her family waited in the car, there was little doubt that the end of summer 1990 was also the end of that relationship.

11

Welcome to the Jungle

Tyler supporting me and my finger tapping, Roxy Theater, Sunset Strip, 1990.

A wise man once told me that, should the Republic of California ever need an enema, the tube is to be inserted in the city of Riverside.

Another one of those cities to the east of Los Angeles, Riverside is home to nearly 300,000 people, a significant part of the urban sprawl local newscasters often refer to as "The Southland." It has a rather historic downtown, a University of California campus, and some of the worst smog in the nation.

Yet in 1990, Riverside also had a legendary club called Spanky's Café, where, on Saturday, October 6, Onyxx played its first headlining slot.

The headliner came on at either 10:00 or 11:00, depending on the number of bands playing that night. Typically, the opening band would come on at 8:00. Openers were always some new/crappy band—usually us. The 9:00 band was known as the supporting act, someone slightly more known, with some kind of following. There was always the possibility of a second supporting slot, but usually the headliners came on at 10:00. Finally, there would be the late-night closing act, whom I rarely stayed around to see.

When your band was headlining, it was your show. The crowd that showed up was there to see you. If no one showed up, then they didn't show up because of you. A club owner was therefore putting faith in you by booking you as headliner, as no people meant no sales at the bar, which is how many clubs make money.

With our fame growing from our shows at Rock Around the Clock, we were able to make the leap to the headlining slot at Spanky's, and were thrilled, even if it had to be in Riverside. It was a good warm up to determine whether or not we were truly prepared for our impending debut on The Strip. For us, headlining Spanky's was like being picked for the varsity baseball team. But the real dream was to get drafted by a minor league team, and for us that was headlining a show on The Strip, at The Whisky or The Roxy. That was where you got recognized by the Big League squads and that's where you landed that holy of holies, the record contract.

Barbi was clearly pointing us in the right direction. In addition to the show at Spanky's and our imminent debut as openers on The Strip the following week, she had set up the Onyxx hotline, which also happened to be her home phone. With ads consistently running in *Screamer*, people actually started calling. Not only for bookings, but for tickets and even the T-shirts onto which we'd had the Onyxx band photo silk-screened and that sold for $10 each (plus shipping and handling). Any money that we saw, which was never much, went into paying for more T-shirts to be made, more ads to be placed in *Screamer*, and more pay-to-play fees. Yet the Spanky's gig would illustrate that, beyond being ready for our Strip debut, Onyxx had made the kind of intangible leap toward rock superstardom that simply does not show up via such material indicators.

Spanky's was one of the few clubs we ever played that was twenty-one and over. The club owners allowed us in provided we didn't come anywhere near the bar. The problem, of course, was that we couldn't rely on our standard teenaged fan base to fill the place up. We had no idea, then, who might show, aside from Baby and some of the other "girls" we'd given tickets to, and we approached the show with the attitude that it would be good practice, if nothing less.

On the night of the show, we were surprised to find that the bar was tightly packed with more than one hundred people. Because of the size of the club, and because we didn't really know any of its temporary occupants, there was a kind of buzz about the show as the two opening acts went through their sets. We waited in the alley out back, as invisibility would clearly create a higher sense of anticipation and create that much more of a sense of relief once we appeared and busted into our opening chords.

As 10:00 approached and the supporting act finished up, Russo and our other roadie, another friend from school named Sam, set up our gear on stage, another ploy to add to the band's mystique.

Aura sufficiently established, we needed only to storm the stage and stake our claim as official headliners. Just before we went on, however, Russo came back, his mouth tight with concern.

"There's something wrong," he said, running a hand through his hair. "Your amp's not working."

I felt the cold rush of panic through my stomach. I ran through a checklist with him: cables running from the amp head to the speaker cabinet? Check. Effects pedals running through the amp? Check. Guitar cable running into effects pedals? Check.

"Is it plugged in?"

He nodded.

Shit. I rushed inside. The place was swarming with people I'd never seen before, peppered with a few familiar faces attached to bodies I wasn't used to seeing quite so clothed. When they saw me they began to murmur and hum, as we were already late coming on (another ploy to create anticipation). I ran through everything one more time and turned my amp on and off. Then Russo noticed something that only a highly proficient guitar tech might notice.

"Your amp's smoking, dude."

Sure enough, billowing from the back of the amp was a healthy stream of smoke, and not the good kind that precedes some kind of cool pyrotechnic. KISS was not about to appear through the mist for a surprise performance. This was a terrible kind of smoke and carried with it the aroma of catastrophe.

Barbi came over, calm. "What's the problem?"

I pointed to the smoke signal being emitted from my amp. It was whispering, "Help."

"Relax," Barbi told me. "We'll handle it." She coolly walked away as my entire body began to sweat. What was I going to do? Cancel the gig? Give these people their money back? We'd never get asked to headline a show again. And the ladies . . . What would the ladies think? They'd see us for the frauds we were. Just kids! We couldn't live up to the ages printed on our fake IDs! We had no business being here! In a twenty-one and over club! Headlining a show!! In Riverside!!!

Just then I felt a supportive hand on my shoulder. I looked up, and standing above me . . .

. . . was Slash. Lead guitarist of Guns N' Roses.

It wasn't really Slash, of course. But it was Slash. A rock 'n' roll guardian angel sent to take care of me in my time of need. Whoever he was, he was the guitarist in one of the other bands, but he had the big afro, no shirt, ratty leather pants, and his voice sounded just like Slash's. I had never met this man before, yet I knew immediately that he was a kindred spirit, a brother in rock, undoubtedly another victim of our fantastic affliction, and therefore he'd come to my rescue.

"Bro," Slash/Not Slash said. "Problems?"

"Yes, Slash. You have to help me."

"I'm not Slash, but I can help you."

He looked over my amp, turned it on, and breathed in the smoke like a sommelier, swishing it around thoughtfully. Then he pronounced his diagnosis.

"Bro. Your amp's fucked."

"I know, Slash! What can I do?"

"I'm not Slash." He looked around for a moment, then back at me. "Use mine."

Russo and one of Slash/Not Slash's roadies came up carrying either end of an amp, followed by Barbi. The amp was a Marshall half-stack, not much different from the one the real Slash uses.

As Russo plugged my guitar in and handed it to me, I was almost moved to tears. I gave Slash/Not Slash an extra-firm handshake and wanted to give him a hug, but he was still glistening with stage sweat, so I thought better of it.

"Rock on," Slash/Not Slash said and left the stage.

I didn't plug in any of my effects. I just used the distortion on the Marshall, one of the purest sounds in all of rock. I nodded to my bandmates, and we kicked into "Rise High."

The show was a smash, or so it seemed in relation to the potential disaster, and no one was more impressed than Baby and the friends we'd made at the strip clubs. In fact, seeing another guitarist loan me his equipment may have even added to our mystique, providing us a kind of credence with the audience that our look, clothing, and stage presence could never have.

It's one thing to headline a show, sign autographs, or even have groupies. It's quite another to be accepted into the camaraderie that is rock guitar musicianhood and have another guitarist, someone who could actually play, recognize you as one of his own and offer salvation in a time of need. It seemed to me the sort of thing Richie Sambora would have done for Skid Row's Dave "The Snake" Sabo, despite the fact that Mr. Sambora had replaced Mr. Sabo in Bon Jovi. The Brotherhood just carried with it that level of absolution. It was a kind of acceptance that I had never experienced elsewhere—not in sport, not in my relationship with Shannon, and certainly not at school. And it also made me believe, more than any of those other perks of being a rock star could, that Onyxx had ascended to an entirely new level of triumph.

We left the stage to the cheers of the crowd, and while the rest of the band mingled, I looked for my guardian angel to thank him again and to introduce him to some of my friends. Maybe he would hit it off with one of Baby's friends and we could all party together. Maybe we could set up another show with his band. Maybe he could come over to my folks' house for spaghetti one night.

I headed through the back door into the alley to find Russo and Slash/Not Slash's roadie shuffling past me with the Marshall. They slid the amp into a white van and slammed the doors shut. Alas, Slash/Not Slash was nowhere to be found. The van pulled away and I never saw that band or my savior again.

Slash/Not Slash expected nothing from me. This is just what axmen in legitimate bands did for each other. Loaned out equipment. Traded guitar licks. Went to Morocco together on holiday and swapped wives. No big deal.

Standing in a back alley in Riverside, it occurred to me that Onyxx was indeed prepared for our debut on The Strip a few weeks later. We'd headlined a gig and averted near-disaster. A&R reps were coming to our shows, as were people we didn't even know. All the suffering and humiliations we'd experienced were just there to keep us grounded, preparing us for membership in the elusive club of the rock 'n' roll star.

With two more shows in less than a week, one on Thursday night at Rock Around the Clock and our debut on The Strip at The Roxy the following Saturday, I had problems that even my newfound status couldn't alleviate.

For one thing, as Slash/Not Slash had so eloquently put it, my amp was fucked, bro. And a guitarist without an amp before his debut on The Strip is like a singer with no voice before her debut on Broadway. Had I actually been a guitar god, I undoubtedly would have had an endorsement from Carvin amplifiers and been provided with a new one before every show. As lead guitarist of Onyxx, however, I had to take my amp into some techs in some warehouse in Fullerton who didn't know who in the hell I was. Perhaps Slash/Not Slash forgot to forward my membership card to them. They could have my amp fixed in time for our upcoming shows, they told me, but it was going to cost me. This was a familiar phrase to those of us who suffer our particular affliction.

Yet even darker clouds loomed on the horizon than my amplifier problems. When my father learned that I was playing a show on a Thursday night, which he, unlike me, apparently still viewed as a school night, he kind of lost his shit at the dinner table. With his insistence that I cancel, it became clear to me that my father didn't realize with whom he was sharing a bubbling pot of fondue.

It turned into a massive blowout about priorities and the fact that, he believed, I looked like a girl. I did not, for the record, look like a girl. "Girl" implies a certain softness of features and innocence of spirit. I looked like an old woman whose hair had experienced one too many calamities.

The real problem, I imagine, was that all the thoughts and feelings that had been building up in my dad during the previous months—as my look became more a part of my life, I stayed out later, and my grades dipped toward mediocrity—had percolated long enough.

My father told me of his days growing up in 1950s Southern California. He was the yo-yo champion of Glendale and drove a 1950 Merc, the same car James Dean drove in *Rebel Without a Cause*. He had, he always told me, a wonderful high school experience, with football games, school dances, and lettermen's jackets, and he wanted the same for me.

I was having my own experience, I told him, without

going into too much detail, and there was nothing he could do to stop me. This was true, incidentally, but probably not the right thing to say just then.

I slammed my fork down and stormed away from the dinner table, as any rock star would, only to find that my dad was chasing after me. As I reached the stairs and began my ascent, I made it about three steps up before my dad grabbed my leg and pulled me back down. He stood above me, cheeks and eyes bulging with rage, my mom shrieking something nonsensical in the background, and I can only imagine what was going through my father's head.

That fall, the country was on the verge of its biggest recession since the Great Depression, and no one was getting hit harder than people who had anything to do with real estate in Southern California. The neon fuel of the Reagan '80s had burnt out, fading away into the colorless term of George H. W. Bush. My dad knew he was going to lose his job shortly thereafter (which he did). He knew his marriage of thirty years was disintegrating (which it was). He had one son who was drinking himself to senselessness and had been kicked out of the Navy for doing so, and now me taking to it (he'd found me vomiting in a hedge), getting calls at 3:00 A.M. from strippers named Baby, and losing sight of what he felt should have been my focus: school.

But instead of giving me the beating I so richly deserved, my father dropped his fist, turned me over . . .

. . . and gave me a good spanking.

"Ah," I thought as my dad paddled my ass. "If only the girls at Spanky's could see me now."

12

Sunset and Babylon

Onyxx made its debut on the Sunset Strip on Saturday, October 13, at 8:00 P.M. The show featured the same lineup as the one at Rock Around the Clock, with Swingin' Thing headlining and Baron Von Rock in the supporting slot. Except that this wasn't Rock Around the Clock. This was The Roxy; this was The Strip.

Sitting in the cramped backstage upstairs, my head between my knees as I sprayed Aqua Net on the undergrowth of my hair (this is how you make it poofy without making it look sticky), I couldn't help but think about the other hair that had been primped in that exact spot or the other famous feet that had stepped on that stage.

In the strictest terms, the Sunset Strip is the area of Sunset Boulevard between Doheny on the west and San

Vicente on the east. Between this quarter-mile strip sat the principal venues of the Hair Metal movement, The Whisky a Go-Go, The Roxy Theater, Gazzarri's (which has sadly been replaced with a Times Squarish monstrosity called The Key Club), and The Rainbow Bar and Grill.

The Strip is often extended south, down Doheny to Doug Weston's Troubadour on Santa Monica Boulevard, and east, to the Coconut Teazer at Crescent Heights and the Cathouse, which was co-owned by *Headbanger's Ball* host Riki Rachtman and Faster Pussycat frontman Taime Downe.

The Sunset Strip is an essential artery in the history of Los Angeles, indeed of entertainment and celebrity as a whole. The Strip gave birth to "Over the Rainbow" and Marilyn Monroe, and it's where John Belushi and River Phoenix died. The Strip's history is one that begins long before the days of patent leather, lace, and suede. It begins in Los Angeles's ancient past: the 1920s.

While gambling was illegal within the City of Angels, it was allowed in Los Angeles County. What became known as The Strip was actually in West Hollywood, out-side Los Angeles city limits, so it became host to gambling parlors and speakeasies frequented by movie stars with loose morals.

From 1928 through 1959, at the far eastern border of The Strip, sat The Garden of Allah hotel and villas, which was home to Humphrey Bogart, Errol Flynn, Greta Garbo, the Marx Brothers, Dorothy Parker, and F. Scott Fitzgerald, who had a heart attack at Schwab's Drug Store across the street while buying a pack of cigarettes.

By the 1960s, the movie stars and literary figures

cashing in on Hollywood had moved on, and the area became a haven to the counterculture. On January 11, 1964, The Whisky opened in a space that had been a bank. While there was always a live band on stage at The Whisky in the '60s, the real attraction came between sets, when a short-skirted DJ played records from a cage suspended just above the stage. When the band came back on, this DJ would dance in the cage, and thus go-go dancing was born.

In addition to being where The Byrds and The Doors were discovered, The Whisky also witnessed the American debuts of British acts like Led Zeppelin, The Who, and The Kinks.

In other words, I, Craig A. Williams, have played on the same stage as Jimmy Paige, Pete Townsend, and Ray Davies.

In the 1970s, The Roxy Theater opened a few blocks east of The Whisky in the location of what had been a strip club. It was host to John Lennon's famed "lost weekend," and it was the West Coast hub of the emerging punk and New Wave scenes.

In other words, I've sprayed my hair with Aqua Net in the same spot that a Beatle, if not THE Beatle, tried to kill himself with heroin while Keith Moon and Alice Cooper helped.

Down at The Troubadour, there was much more of a folk feel. Some of the people who made names for themselves on the stage of that venue include Neil Diamond, Bruce Springsteen, and Elton John.

In other words . . . Well, I was pretty stoked.

The Strip became synonymous with Hair Metal once

Bill Gazzarri opened his eponymous club in the late 1970s. The scene began with Van Halen, who were followed in the early 1980s by acts like W.A.S.P., Mötley Crüe, and Ratt. By the mid 1980s, The Strip was the heart of American pop culture. It was excessive and absurd, but undeniably significant. Consider that more than 130 million albums were sold by Van Halen (57 million), Guns N' Roses (38 million), the Crüe (24 million), and Poison (14 million) alone. And they all started at one of these clubs along this stretch of Sunset. As a result, kids from all over the world descended on the scene, forming bands that tried to outdo their predecessors with bigger hair, more makeup, and more ridiculous costuming. Some hoped to make it, some hoped to help others make it, and some hoped only to watch.

On any given night throughout the 1980s and early 1990s, The Strip was clogged with long-haired, leather-clad, cowboy-booted "musicians" *on foot* (this is noteworthy in Southern California) who handed out fluorescent fliers advertising their upcoming shows. These fliers littered the sidewalks and were pasted to walls and lampposts, while every few feet, teenaged girls in miniskirts asked for autographs or photos.

And it wasn't just the fans congregating on this little stretch of road that provided its energy. Most nights, you'd see the gods themselves, who were always shorter than I expected them to be. When I saw Tracii Guns outside The Roxy, he only came up to my shoulder, although, to be fair, the heels on my boots were substantial. Taime Downe, to paraphrase *Fletch*, was maybe five and a half feet tall, but almost six feet with his teased hair.

Slash and Duff lived up to their godlike status, mostly because I couldn't get close enough to them because of the mob that surrounded them as they walked west on Sunset one evening. Yet another time, I saw Mr. W. Axl Rose himself, in the passenger seat of a BMW, window rolled down, enjoying a cigarette and a moment of anonymity. Then someone screamed "Axl!" and The Strip went nuts. I saw him mouth the words *ah fuck* and roll up the window. The driver of the BMW tried to speed away, but by then the car was mobbed.

Most of these rock stars were departing or arriving at the rock 'n' roll lounge that was The Rainbow Bar and Grill. Adjacent to The Roxy, The Rainbow was to butt rockers what Haight-Ashbury was to hippies. In the video for Guns N' Roses's "November Rain," The Rainbow is the setting for the fistfight between Stephanie Seymour and the other hot model who's trying to steal Axl away from her. The Rainbow is the inspiration for W.A.S.P.'s "Sunset and Babylon," when Blackie Lawless croons, "In here's the land of sun and sin/All the freaks here gonna let you in." The Rainbow was a gathering place for heavy metal debauchery, with sex in booths, under tables, in bathrooms, or in any dark corner.

Such decadence spread throughout The Strip. Who *hadn't* had sex in the bathroom at The Whisky (Tyler apparently had—with my ex, Shannon) or along the long, dark stretch of Doheny down toward The Troubadour? Even before our debut on The Strip, Onyxx was often recognized while passing out fliers there. Young women who had seen our ads in *Screamer* would run up to us in small packs for an autograph and a photo, which occasionally led to some form of debauchery in some dark corner of The Strip.

Eventually, the procession would lead to the clubs themselves. Once inside The Whisky, The Roxy, The Troubadour, or Gazzarri's, throngs nodded their heads and swayed to bands with names like Gang Bang or Legs Up, hoping that they were watching the births of bands that someday might be somewhat famous.

And had they been at The Roxy on October 13, 1990, at 8:00 P.M., they would have seen teen Glam Metal sensations Onyxx.

As the stage went black and a cheer went up from the capacity crowd, Onyxx huddled backstage. We'd begun to do this before shows to get one another pumped up. We'd join hands and say inspirational things to one another, such as, "Let's have a kick-ass show." Our name was announced over the PA and we rushed down the stairs and stepped onto the stage, our arms raised high in triumph.

The front rows were jammed with young ladies we'd never seen before. Behind them were people we'd met at various locations (strip clubs, malls, restaurants, and along Sunset as we handed out fliers), and some of the audience had just seen our ad or heard about us through a friend. It was our biggest crowd yet.

In the middle of the room were some familiar faces from school, good friends to be sure, and, in the back, in a sectioned-off "VIP area," were my parents. Barbi had reserved a table for them.

Having grown up with John Hughes's films, I wish I could tell you that once the show was over and we left the stage to the chanting and cheering of our growing fan base, there was a tearful moment between my father and me. As though, having finally seen what it was that I had committed my time and energy to and realized that I was actually good at it, he would push his way backstage to find me, sweating and exhausted from leaving my heart out there for my fans. Maybe there would be an awkward moment as he gazed at me proudly from across the room, his eyes welling up with tears. Maybe I'd whisper something like "Hey, Pop. Catch the show?" And maybe he would rush over and embrace me, telling me how proud he is of his rock star son.

But that didn't happen.

As soon as our set was over, and it was a helluva set, we took off for the Travelodge on Sunset and Highland, where we'd booked a room that we had stocked with as much booze as Barbi could get her hands on so that we could spend time with our fans and get to know them better. We managed to squeeze a good fifty people or so into that room, but the fit was lubricated with plenty of liquor. We enjoyed a tighter fit in the hotel closet with a couple of groupies, yet another amenity of playing The Strip.

Groupies became a regular occurrence from that day forward. Usually these groupies were sets of girls, from their late teens to early twenties, who had come to our shows, approached us afterward, and asked us where our afterparty was. Fortunately, by then we were smart enough to have an answer for them. And if there was anything we learned from Great White's groupies, it was that a hotel room was the foundation of any decent afterparty.

But having groupies is just part of the DNA of a rock star, like shiny hair or an addictive personality. As primitive rock god and wise forefather Gene Simmons says, "Being a rock star and bragging about getting laid is like turning on a faucet and bragging about finding water." While I can't say I ever quite got that used to the groupies, they weren't as difficult to deal with as, say, biology class, either.

By the time I made it back home the day after my triumph on The Strip, bleary-eyed yet invigorated by the sheer potential of life, I found my dad in his bedroom, paying bills.

"Hey. What'd you think?"

"We all had a great time," he told me, trying to suppress a laugh. And failing at it.

When I pressed him on it, he couldn't hold back.

He thought we were terrible. He thought we were so terrible that he supposed we were trying to be bad, as an experiment, to see if people would still come. In retrospect, I actually wish I'd thought of the postmodern take on it, but, alas, it wasn't the case. We were actually trying.

While The Roxy may have been our debut on The Strip, it was the last time my parents would ever see me perform. For both of them, seeing me up on stage might have given them stage fright.

Fortunately, they hadn't seen me off stage.

13

Too Young to Fall in Love

Ready to rock around the clock, Montclair, 1990.

In addition to the joy of groupies and the historical reverence aroused by playing on The Strip, it suddenly became easier for Onyxx to get gigs off The Strip. Club owners actually asked us to play as opposed to Barbi having to constantly push for us. The pay-to-play concept always applied, but now we were receiving calls from club owners and promoters wanting to take our money.

One exception to the pay-to-play rule was yet another obscure club in the Valley called Rock Haven. Despite the

160

fact that the club was a two-hour drive from our Orange County homes, we made the trip north one Sunday afternoon shortly after our triumph at The Roxy. The club was small, with semicircular booths set into the walls and a small dance floor at the foot of a small stage. Seeing a nightclub in the daylight was rather depressing, like seeing your grandparents naked.

We were greeted at the door by the club owner, a Persian man wearing a white suit and white hat. On either arm was a young lady in a short frayed denim skirt and a tube top. He hugged Barbi, as they had apparently met before, shook each of our hands, and introduced us to "his daughters." He winked at us here, the girls laughed, and we all tried not to skip over to one of the booths.

He wanted us to play his club next Saturday, he told us, his arm now slung around Barbi.

"That's not enough time for us to promote," we said. "And this place is far. We'd definitely need a hotel room."

He nodded. "I get you guys hotel room." We looked at Barbi, who seemed surprised, too. "And limo, from hotel to club."

This was sounding good, and we all exchanged looks. He took our looks to be hesitation, so he went for the hard sell.

"You like tits?"

We indicated that, indeed, we did.

"Look at these." He reached over and pulled down one of the young ladies' tube top. She laughed, pushed her breasts together, and set them on the table. I hoped they'd clean that spot before they served someone a salad later. The other girl then pulled her top down, too, and mirrored her "sister's" actions.

But the boob show was merely ornamentation as he leaned in for his final offer.

"I get you guys all blow jobs."

That Saturday, once we'd completed our sound check, we drove back to the hotel our benefactor had procured for us, one of those nondescript chain hotels with two or three floors made of beige stucco. The four of us shared a room and, while we got dressed, we decided to have some preshow cocktails, assuming vodka in red plastic cups can be considered "cocktails." Once the vodka kicked in and we were glammed up, we had a little acoustic jam session to warm up for the gig until the limo the owner had promised us arrived.

Mid-song, there was a knock on the door. We assumed it was security responding to complaints of noise, so we stashed the liquor under the bed.

When we opened the door, though, we found a thin, shirtless black man panting in the doorway.

"Y'all musicians?"

I held my guitar up, nodded.

"I play sax!"

"Me, too!" Actually, I hadn't touched a sax in close to three years, but I doubted this man would have access to my school records.

We invited him in and offered him a drink. As he sat on the bed, sipping his plastic cup of vodka, he told us, "I was next door, hittin' it with my lady . . ." Here, he pantomimed what he'd been doing up to about three minutes before. I thought about how I'd just shook his hand, but vodka makes you shrug.

He continued, ". . . When I heard singing. I was like, 'Damn, baby! We got us some musicians next door!'"

We all laughed.

"So who are you guys?"

We told him all about Onyxx, our show that night, and the glory of the Glam Metal movement as a whole.

"I don't listen to that shit. Y'all famous?"

Not yet, we told him, but it was just a matter of time.

He thought a moment, sipped his vodka, and then looked up, inspired. "I could play sax on your album!"

We didn't really have a part for sax, we told him, but if we needed one, we'd come find him. He then told us his name and where he lived.

The limo pulled up to take us back to the club and we all walked outside, as though this was how we always traveled to our shows.

He looked at the car, then back at us. "Who *are* you guys really?"

I paused at the stairwell and looked him in the eye. "We're rock stars, sir."

After the show, which maybe five people came to, including the two girls in the tube tops and a corpulent waitress Kyle had met at the Mexican restaurant where we'd had pregig supper, we rode back to the hotel in the limo with Barbi, where she'd booked a room as well.

Turned out, while we were getting ready for our lame

gig, Barbi was having dinner with the Persian club owner. He had propositioned her in various ways, she told us, saying that he would take care of her for the rest of his life. The show, the limo, and the hotel, it occurred to me, had all been a form of babysitting.

"Sssso," Kyle furrowed his brow, "so all this was just so he could . . ." his jaw moved around in circles, a new technique his therapist had given him. "So he could get in your pants?"

Barbi smiled and shrugged. "I guess."

"Shit," Kyle said. "Doesn't he know it's easier than that?"

We all laughed. Kyle was kidding. Of course.

Later that night, the four members of Onyxx partied in our hotel room with the tube top girls, the waitress from the Mexican restaurant, and Barbi. We would have invited our saxophone-playing neighbor and his lady friend, but they had apparently checked out. At some point, what had been a moderately crowded room suddenly felt less so. Tyler noticed first.

"Where did Barbi and Sonny go?"

Being that there weren't too many places they could have been hiding within the confines of our room, we all rushed out on the balcony that overlooked the pool/hot tub area. It was late, so it was empty. A cloud of steam rose from the hot tub. Through that steam, in the still of the night, we could make out two naked figures, one as dark as the other was pale. A yin. And a yang.

On the concrete edge of the hot tub, we saw our thirty-eight-year-old manager and sixteen-year-old bass player, exposed, entwined, hands roaming, lips locked. World upended.

Apparently, we had a groupie from within.

Sonny was constantly in love with someone, which isn't necessarily a bad quality as much as it is a treacherous one. Particularly for a bass player.

The bass is the core of the song, its most fundamental part, and therefore it must be passionless, never persuaded by the lyric of the singer, the riff of the guitarist, or the occasional abuse of the cowbell by the percussionist. The bass player's duty is to hold a song together, fastening all the parts with those thick, significant strings, much like the current theory as to the fundamental makeup of the universe. Without bass, it is presumed, there can be only chaos.

But Sonny was a romantic and there was always someone to whom he was professing his devotion. This didn't take away from his abilities as a bass player; he was probably the best practitioner of his instrument in the band. But his passion made him unsatisfied with the role to which that instrument relegated him, craving the attention usually reserved for the other musicians.

Of course, many bass players find their way into the limelight. Paul McCartney played bass, as did Gene Simmons and Steve Harris, who wrote much of the music for KISS and Iron Maiden, respectively. But McCartney also sang and played guitar, Gene Simmons sang and vomited blood, and no one outside of me and a few other recovering rock stars knows who in the hell Steve Harris is (and those who have not heard of the man should be ashamed of themselves).

Given Sonny's place in the band, he obviously needed some outlet for his passions. I just don't think any of us suspected that outlet to be on top of, underneath, or even behind a Loni Anderson impersonator.

There is absolutely nothing that can break up a band faster than when one member of the band engages in an affair that the rest of the band doesn't approve of. Nothing, that is, unless you add in the fact that the woman involved in the affair also happens to be the band's manager. And happens to be two-and-a-half times older than the band member with whom she's engaging in such passions. And her daughters go to high school with the boy. I don't mean to sound like a Puritan on this one, but such an affair does tend to curdle the proverbial band milk.

It didn't occur to me at the time just how depraved Barbi's affair with Sonny was, which I can attribute only to the naivety caused both by my youth and my affliction. While Sonny maintains to this day that intercourse never occurred, there are obvious statutory and ethical issues involved with this turn of events.

Initially, Sonny's crush had been more banal, having focused his affections on Barbi's oldest daughter, Robin. Sonny had pursued Robin as a sleepy kind of admirer. I'd see them talking together in the halls at school, they'd go to movies together, and Sonny spent a lot of time at the condo studying with her. Nothing ever came from his pursuits, as Robin viewed him as more of a good friend than as the lover he undoubtedly assured her he could be.

His heart was broken one evening at a band meeting during which, somehow, we got drunk while talking about upcoming shows, promotions, and when we might record a demo. That night, Tyler made out simultaneously with Robin and a cheerleader friend she'd invited over. A mere knowledge of this would have been enough to crush Sonny's soul, but Tyler made a point of doing it under the dining room table, where we could all see them.

It was an inexplicably cruel act on Tyler's part, which is of course why he'd done it. We all knew of Sonny's feelings for Robin, and it was not as though she was a knockout who was irresistible to the teen gigolo that was Tyler. But it was precisely because of his knowledge of Sonny's feelings for Robin that Tyler was compelled to do it. As a result, Sonny spent the rest of the evening in a melodramatic haze, pulling from a bottle of vodka while muttering, "See what you did, Robin? You drove me to the bottle."

Rebuffed by the daughter, Sonny's affections were then secretly transferred to Barbi, a fact made apparent on the occasion of seeing them dry hump just outside a hot tub at a chain hotel in the northern reaches of the San Fernando Valley.

For Barbi's part, she approached me about this incident later, like a contrite daughter, claiming to have no recollection of making out with Sonny. I'm not convinced that "I was drunk and blacked out" is a valid excuse when a group of minors is placed in your ward and you attempt to asphyxiate one of them with your tongue. But she promised me it would never happen again, and, to my knowledge, it didn't. With Sonny.

Sonny, simple as it sounds, just wanted to be loved, and he needed a friend within the framework of the band. Not only did he look different than the rest of us, which is a dangerous thing when you're a teenager, but his sensitivity made him an easy and worthwhile target for our teasing. For the most part, our pestering had always been good natured, the sort of goading that teenage boys engage in as a way of killing any kind of spirit or individuality. Yet Sonny was a bold steed and couldn't be broken, which meant only that our ribbing grew increasingly malicious as the years went by.

I suppose then that Sonny initially gravitated toward Barbi for a kind of protection from the rest of us. Ultimately, romantic feelings developed, and once he acted on those feelings, it created a rift that, as time went on, would prove fatal to Onyxx.

Perhaps if Sonny had owned up to the absurdity of the affair, or even laughed about it with the rest of the band, we might have laid off. But Sonny's reaction was to ignore us with indignation, as though he were a part of something much more sophisticated than the rest of us could comprehend.

As a result, we began spending less and less time with Sonny outside of rehearsal. It was always Kyle, Tyler, and I going out to Cloud 9 at Knott's Berry Farm or Videopolis, an outdoor dance club at Disneyland, where we'd utilize our rock star image to seduce unsuspecting tourists and see how far we could get with them on the Peter Pan ride.

Meanwhile, Sonny got more involved in areas outside of the band. At school, he joined Key Club, where his acts of philanthropy led to him befriending members of a local church youth group. He spent more and more of his time with this youth group, taking white-water rafting trips and learning to play U2 and Bon Jovi songs on an acoustic guitar under the moonlight of the Klamath River. This had two effects.

First, the rest of the band of course made fun of Sonny for spending all his time with youth ministers and dialoguing about the Lord, and this lengthened the divide.

The second, and much more significant, effect of Sonny's white-water crusades was that he began writing his own songs.

The history of Onyxx's songwriting was simple. I'd write a song, teach the parts to Sonny and Kyle, and then as we went through it a couple times, they'd sort of improvise and make those parts their own. I always had the final say on what stayed and what went, although keeping control of Kyle's drumming was often like trying to wrangle a manatee. A fight would usually break out between Kyle and Sonny, as Sonny would accuse Kyle of being inconsistent with his kick drum. Which he was.

As bass player and drummer, Sonny and Kyle were the rhythm section of Onyxx. It was crucial that Kyle's kick drum meld with Sonny's bass line for the music to sound unified, thoughtful, and (most important for a rhythm section) rhythmic. But no two people in the band hated each other more than Sonny and Kyle. Rather than them coming to any kind of accord and the band actually sounding tight, Kyle would usually conclude the argument by throwing one of his drumsticks at Sonny's head and storming out of the rehearsal room.

While we were working on the music, Tyler would listen in a corner, writing lyrics and a melody in his head. He rarely wrote the lyrics down, and as time went on, I began to believe that he'd make most of them up as he went along. There are parts in surviving recordings from the era that would support this argument. This method was, along with virtually every other facet of Onyxx, limiting.

Once the music was set, and Tyler had retrieved Kyle from the parking lot, where he'd sulk about what a dick Sonny was, Tyler would grab his microphone, sing over what we had, and the song would evolve from there. This is the way it had been since "Sun Angel," and I was quite keen on keeping it this way.

When our debut album eventually came out, I wanted the insert to read, "All songs written by Williams." I had already ceded enough creative control to Tyler by allowing him to write the lyrics, so I might consider sharing a small amount of credit with him. But then Sonny had to come in with his *Rattle and Hum* and *The Joshua Tree* acoustic youth group horseshit and shake things up.

I showed up to Bands West one day after school for rehearsal, and Sonny was already in the studio, alone, with his own guitar. And not a bass, but a six-string acoustic that I wasn't even aware he had. I watched him through the small window in the door that looked into the studio. He was perched on the drum riser, eyes closed, singing with supreme confidence a tune I had never heard before. And not badly, either.

I didn't allow my presence to be known to Sonny. Instead, I crept away and waited outside for Tyler and Kyle to get there so that we could make fun of him together, as a band. As we all know, this is the healthiest way to disarm something that threatens you.

As soon as Tyler and Kyle pulled up, I told them what I had seen and heard, and they rushed into the studio to see and hear for themselves. We all gathered around the door to listen, and Sonny was still going at it. But instead of bursting out in laughter, as I'd somehow hoped, they nodded their heads a little, then pulled the door open. Sonny immediately stopped and looked up, guilty, anticipating an earful of shit.

In place of said earful of shit, though, Tyler sat down next to him on the drum riser, fascinated.

"Play it again," he told him.

Sonny did. It was a song called "In Your Heart," a simple acoustic ballad that I didn't see how I fit into at all.

Given his recent actions with Barbi, it wasn't surprising that the song was about a boy and the dangers of a clandestine love affair. Should the boy act upon such an affair, he would, it appeared, become a vague sort of nomadic pyromaniac.

VERSE

Feelings burn inside,
Oh yeah.
I don't want to play with fire tonight.

That boy plays with fire.
That boy he plays with fire.
But you'd better watch your step boy,
'Cause it's a long and winding,
Long and winding,
Long and winding road.

The chorus then acknowledges how such a nefarious enterprise should be dealt with: Simply walk away from it. While the passion could never be realized in a physical manner, it could live on in the subject's heart:

So long, babe.
Don't forget about me,
Don't cry, babe,
I'll be in your heart tonight.

Sonny sang it the same way he had when he thought he was alone. When he finished, Tyler and Kyle nodded. They turned to me, where I leaned up against the mirrored wall of the studio, arms folded, a sour look on my face.

"What do you think?" they asked me.

I thought it was cute. Now could we please rehearse my songs?

But Tyler wasn't done. "I think we should add it to the set."

Kyle concurred, humming the chorus to himself as he set up his drum kit.

I, on the other hand, thought this was the worst idea since Sabbath agreed to kick out Ozzy. For one thing, the chord structure was a rip-off of "Every Rose Has Its

Thorn." Is that what we really wanted? To be some Poison knockoff? Secondly, the melody was lifted from L.A. Guns's magnificent power ballad "The Ballad of Jayne." Not derivative, mind you. It was the same song.

I pleaded my case, red-faced, frustrated that I had to point out something so obvious to my bandmates, as though one of them had suddenly become enamored with Wilson Phillips and I had to explain to them why "Hold On" sucked. Never, however, did I let on as to what my real problem with Sonny's song had been.

It wasn't mine.

The other issues were irrelevant, if not hypocritical. Every song I had ever written had been an accident while trying to figure out some other band's song. Everything about our band was somewhere between derivative and Xerox. Even so, I wanted to be the creative center of the band—its purpose. I wanted to be the *y* in Onyxx.

Unfortunately, I was outvoted, as though my band were suddenly a democracy, and rehearsal that afternoon consisted of Sonny teaching Tyler the lyrics to his song while I sulked in the corner. I wrote a begrudging guitar solo for the beginning and middle parts of the song, hoping they'd all wake up the next day and realize what a horrible mistake they were making.

They didn't, of course, and not only was the song made part of our set, it became one of our most popular. It was simple and audiences could sing along to it, as though they'd heard it before, and that made it a hit.

We never stopped giving Sonny shit, of course, but he was now emboldened. A few weeks later, he came into the studio with another acoustic number, this one called

"Chances." The theme of "Chances" was, not surprisingly, secret love and disappearing with a secret lover to "a place far away" in order to consummate the heretofore unconsummated affair. Unlike "In Your Heart," however, "Chances" suggested in its chorus that the two lovers take a chance and actually pursue their affair.

VERSE

I wanna run
To a place far away
I wanna hide
And see a brighter day
There's a place for us in Heaven
Just you, and me.
So why don't we go
And have a look, and see.

BRIDGE

I wanna run
I wanna hide
I wanna break down and cry.
'Cause love to me's a two-way street
And I don't know if we're right.

CHORUS

Just give me a chance.

On this tune, Tyler and Sonny shared vocal duties in a call and response fashion, while I disappeared into the back of the stage to smoke a cigarette with Kyle. On stage, I tried to play along as the good guy, the one who didn't always need to be the center of attention. Yet the truth was, playing backup was gnawing at my ego something fierce.

To return my genius to the forefront of Onyxx, I channeled my frustration into a charming little minuet that introduced "Chances" the same way Tesla did with their "Love Song." Even though my latest opus was in a different key than the rest of "Chances," the band went for it and my ego was temporarily sated.

By October of 1990, "In Your Heart" and "Chances" were integral parts of our set, and Sonny had found his way into the hearts of his own set of fans. Some of them were people from his youth group and some were friends of his younger sister. What were the chances, though, that the biggest fan of Sonny's tunes would be our thirty-eight-year-old manager?

As it would turn out, pretty good.

14

More Than Words

There are three types of news events that clutch the interest of residents of the greater Anaheim Hills/Yorba Linda area.

At the top of the list is the natural disaster. The earthquake, sure, but that's rare and even more rarely is it localized. More often, we're confronted by the brush fire or the landslide (the former usually precedes the latter), and I have terrifying memories of coming back from a soccer game to find my parents chucking items into the back of the family car as helicopters swooped overhead, some godlike voice telling us we had thirty minutes to get out before we and everything we owned was engulfed in flames. It is the closest I have come to being a refugee.

So far. But to live in Southern California is to live with the potential for natural disaster.

The next is the "Local Kid/Celebrity Who Died in Tragic Fashion" story. From the sixth grade on, I don't remember a year in which at least one member of the student body of my school didn't perish in some terrible manner. Drowning, accidental shootings, cancer, a blood clot, car accidents, and being impaled on a gate were just some of the ways children in our area met their all-too-early demise. Every academic year began with an assessment of my peers, wondering who might survive to witness the following summer and who might end up on the back of the wrong Kawasaki Ninja.

The celebrities in this area were almost exclusively athletes, players for the Angels or the Rams who would often set up businesses in the community. Rod Carew's hitting school certainly made sense, Rams's place kicker Tony Zendejas's Mexican restaurant was a noble effort, but there was something depressing about Vince Ferragamo's Touchdown! Real Estate.

Occasionally, though, life defeats these celebrity athletes, as was the case with former Angels relief pitcher Donnie Moore. He had apparently been disintegrating for some time, ever since giving up what erroneously became known as the losing home run in game five of the 1986 American League Championship.

Everyone talks about that year's World Series because it involved yet another Red Sox collapse, but from the point of view of a thirteen-year-old boy in Anaheim, Boston shouldn't have been in that World Series in the first place. Mike Witt was one strike away from his second complete game of the series, but the Angels gave up four runs in the ninth, the last two on a home run while Donnie Moore happened to be on the mound.

Moore never stopped hearing about that home run, and he eventually shot his wife and himself in front of their daughter, who was at the time a senior at my high school. Then, at least, the locals stopped talking about that home run.

What really excites the residents of the eastern Santa Ana Canyon are the "Local Kid Does Good" stories. Again, these stories usually focused on an athlete who won a state championship or overcame some handicap to achieve greatness. On November 29, 1990, however, the eyes of the entire canyon fell upon Tyler, Sonny, Kyle, and me when the Orange County edition of the *Los Angeles Times* ran an in-depth exposé of Onyxx.

The article began as a project for a student at Esperanza High who needed an article for her school paper, the *Daily Aztlan*. The author of the piece was a friend of Barbi's daughter Robin, who convinced her friend to write her article about the band her mom was, ahem, managing.

The *Aztlan* printed the story on October 26 with the headline "High School Glam Rock Band Hopes to Take on Hollywood." The article is without irony, focused primarily on Tyler, as he was a student at Esperanza, and how we were trying to overcome the odds and our youthfulness to succeed in the music industry. Our publicity photo accompanies the piece and, while the article is brief, it includes a remarkable amount of Onyxx philosophy and business savvy that was also included in the *Times* piece.

The *Aztlan* was small-time, though, so the author submitted this documentation of delusion for some sort of competition in the *Times* called "High Life, a weekly forum for high school students." Her story was selected and the editor at the *Times* requested that the author expand it a bit.

This young lady asked for yet another interview. In the time since the *Aztlan* article had run, Onyxx had moved from hoping to take on Hollywood to taking it on. To prove it, we gave her a free ticket to come up and see our next show.

A headlining gig.

At The Whisky.

That was sold out.

It was our first headlining gig on The Strip, and selling it out was a sign of the rising status of the band. No longer were we begging classmates to come to our shows; much of our sales were coming via the newly established Onyxx hotline.

Most of our evenings were now spent in West Hollywood, handing out fliers, signing autographs, and having photos snapped with people we didn't know. We could actually walk up to the door of any club on The Strip, nod to the bouncer, and walk in. Onyxx had, as they say, buzz.

With a reporter for the *Los Angeles Times* (despite the fact that she was really a student who wrote for the *Daily Aztlan*) backstage for an interview at a sold-out Whisky a

Go-Go show, something like hubris began to take hold. Unfortunately, none of us had yet read much in the way of classical tragedy. As Tyler pointed out:

> "A lot of people shoot us down because of the way we look, but we seem to do well with the opposite sex and the Hollywood scene."

I even got in the fun:

> "We have a good sense of appeal to record companies. They seem to be looking for New Kids on the Block in metal."

Accompanying the article is a photograph, which takes up almost half the page. It was taken by a photographer for the *Times* who came by the studio one afternoon, much to the surprise of James and everyone else who worked at Bands West.

The photo really tells you everything you need to know about the internal state of the band. Tyler, Kyle, and I are huddled closely together, standing at the foot of the stage in our studio. I am trying to look tough, I think, although it's difficult because my hair is nothing short of pretty. Kyle, yet again, has a smirk on his face, while Tyler looks a little concerned, like maybe he picked the wrong shirt and bandana combination and someone may print this photo of him seventeen years in the future without his permission.

Then there's a significant foot-wide gap between Sonny and me. Sonny's sitting down on the stage, leaning away from the rest of us. Because of the resolution of the photograph, his expression can't quite be deciphered, but there appears to be a sort of smile, as if to say, "Aren't these guys ridiculous?"

To answer his query, the article, which tackled band history, the spontaneity of our image, and the depth of our delusion, provides an irrefutable conclusion: yes.

Any spontaneity to our image mentioned above is as much a piece of fiction as is our alleged planned tour of Japan and Canada. I think, maybe, Barbi had mentioned a show at a place called the Mason Jar in Phoenix—Arizona, not Saskatchewan.

Most curious, though, is Barbi's suggestion in the article that the members of Onyxx could be seen as role models. My problem with this notion was not that our behavior exempted us from role model status, although our conduct certainly was becoming more suspect. After that sold-out show at The Whisky where the author had interviewed us, for example, we were kicked out of a hotel room for the first time. Rather than our usual room at the Travelodge, we took the proceeds from our show to book a room at a place on Sunset, across the street from the infamous Hyatt House. (Read *Hammer of the Gods*, one of the Led Zeppelin biographies, for more on what was known as the "Riot House.")

Allegedly, Kyle had gotten into something of a spat with some of the fellas from the rival teen band Trixter in the lobby of our hotel. We abhorred Trixter's song "Give It to Me Good" and its accompanying video that aired on MTV every twenty-seven minutes. The song was overly simple, we thought, and we hated their sleeveless flannel muscle shirt look.

Someone within our camp took this altercation to mean that Trixter was threatened by Onyxx, the "hair apparent" to teenaged heartthrob metal. In some sort of stupor, we decided that we had to show Trixter we could party harder than anyone. So we packed a hundred people or so into our room, and before we could even get a TV out the window, we were ejected.

Our behavior continued to disintegrate when drugs came into play, although it's difficult to pinpoint exactly when this happened. Weed had always been around, at least since I was twelve and my brother and his girlfriend first got me stoned while watching reruns of *Star Trek*. But I'm talking about real drugs.

Oddly, acid is the first thing I remember Kyle and Tyler bringing to the rehearsal studio one afternoon. Sonny and I were terrified of the tiny tab of paper, but Kyle and Tyler each put one on their tongue. By the end of the afternoon, both of them had pupils the size of dimes and Kyle, while looking at the scruff of his face in the mirror, was convinced spiders had infested his visage and had to be taken home.

Cocaine had found its way into at least a few of our parties, not only from groupies, but also from a group of rich kids Tyler had begun hanging out with who also went to Esperanza. They all had ridiculous names like Chase and Garrett and, much like their female counterparts, simply wanted to party with a group of kids who might be famous. Hell, we'd been in the *Aztlan,* so who knew?

Still, I don't believe any of these factors prohibited Onyxx, necessarily, from being the influential role models Barbi had advertised us to be. Nor was it because I had some moral or social problem with the idea of rock stars being perceived as role models.

No, my problem is that no one really knew who we were, let alone looked up to us, let alone would be influenced by anything we did.

The article also points out that at our last show we autographed more than two hundred of our promotional photos. But we didn't write down any advice. By the end of 1990 we were receiving fan mail, people were ordering our T-shirts, teenage girls were requesting that we make appearances at their birthday parties . . .

We made appearances at teenage girls' birthday parties.

But I'm pretty sure our influence ended as soon as we walked out the door (or, more often, dropped them back at their houses).

Certainly, no one at school saw us as role models. It is true that the day the *Times* article appeared, Sonny and I were a novelty. Several teachers read the article aloud while we suppressed grins behind our bangs. A few teachers even kept the article posted on their walls for the remainder of the school year. Kids I'd never met before came up to me and asked if that was really me in the newspaper. I told them it was, they'd nod, walk away, and that was pretty much it. No member of the student body asked me, as a role model, for relationship advice, and my influence didn't even crack the realm of student body politics.

No Bono was I.

15

Civil War

Sonny, me, and Tyler in Mammoth Lakes, California.

The strangest thing about the free clinic in Santa Ana was the hot dog vendor out front. Located in yet another corporate business park, the atmosphere was almost festive, with kids running around on the grass median that bordered the parking lot and families that seemed to know one another catching up. Perhaps the word *free* puts people in this mood, but the merriment was the one thing at the free clinic that didn't seem contagious.

Kyle came with me to the clinic because I had what looked like the produce section of the grocery store growing on my groin and I needed moral support. I imagine this is unsettling for anyone, but it seemed especially so for someone who had just turned seventeen. The whole thing was antifantasy, and it was a facet of the rock 'n' roll lifestyle that wasn't generally advertised.

Kyle didn't seem nearly as uptight about the whole experience as I, as by this time, Kyle was a bit more experienced. In the early part of 1991, Kyle was apparently expecting his first child.

He found out about his alleged paternity one afternoon during rehearsal. The expectant mother showed up unannounced at Bands West, where we usually refrained from receiving visitors; they tended to distract from the work at hand. So when this woman showed up with a brand new pair of cowboy boots for Kyle, we knew something was up.

She was in her early twenties, another of our pregig waitresses Kyle seemed keen on seducing. She came to the show that night, then back to our hotel room afterward. Kyle saw her for a few months, and then it ended because he grew tired of the long commute to see her.

He hadn't seen her in months, but when she walked into the studio, he crawled out from behind his drum kit and gave her a warm hug.

Kyle pulled away from her and said, "Wwwwwhat's up?"

"Congratulations," she said, handing him the boots and smiling. "You're gonna be a dad!"

The rest of us excused ourselves and took a break outside, but I don't think we resumed rehearsal that day.

To my knowledge, the woman had the child sometime in 1991. Although it was never confirmed that Kyle was the father, it often terrifies me to think of the possibility of some stuttering teenager stumbling around somewhere out there with no sense of rhythm.

Kyle wasn't the only one allegedly spreading his seed. A few months prior, while backstage at a club appropriately called Jezebel's in the unfortunately named Orange County burg of Placentia, a young woman of nineteen or so burst into our dressing room, hysterical and in tears. She was one of scores of women Tyler had slept with in the previous months, and we all froze when we saw her.

"I need to talk to you," she told Tyler, who chomped nonchalantly on a piece of gum.

Tyler looked at all of us, looking at him. "We have a show," he said, and shrugged.

She looked around at the rest of us, who were by now avoiding her gaze. Behind the door, in the main part of the club, *Appetite for Destruction* played over the PA.

"I'm pregnant, you asshole." She burst into tears again, and now the rest of us stared at the floor.

There was a long pause as Tyler watched her, shoulders heaving, wiping tears from her face, but he didn't move. Finally, he said, "What's your name again?"

The woman exploded in a variety of emotions and ran out of the room. While Tyler's paternity was never confirmed, none of us had anything to say to Tyler at that point. We got called out on stage as "Rocket Queen" came to an end out in the main part of the club. We gave quite probably the worst performance we ever gave that night, and as a result set a firm rule for future shows: No club was to play Guns N' Roses over the PA before we came out on stage.

I suppose, then, my crisis was minor. Just a little STD, but that hardly made the free clinic in Santa Ana any more appealing.

As Kyle and I walked in, I was overwhelmed by a hideous smell of antiseptic and fake Drakkar Noir. Babies cried and the fluorescent lighting flickered overhead. I longed for the festive atmosphere out front and retreated.

I took the position that, if I waited long enough, my "problem" might just go away. After several weeks, much to my surprise, it didn't.

Naturally, I became convinced that I had no immune system and, if I could contract one STD, surely I could contract any STD. It became obvious to me, then, that I had been infected with HIV.

HIV wasn't a big topic of conversation on The Strip, not because we weren't aware of it, but because it was still seen as a problem limited to the homosexual community. Butt rockers were about as sensitive to homosexuals as they were to women, as exemplified by the T-shirt worn by Skid Row's Sebastian Bach that read, "AIDS: Kills fags dead." Mr. Bach apologized profusely for the shirt, but songs like Guns N' Roses's "One in a Million" and the complete lack of openly gay rockers (this was before Judas Priest's Rob Halford came out) imply a deep-seeded homophobia that might be expected in a community of what were essentially cross-dressers.

I had received at least a modest amount of "AIDS education" in health class. If nothing less, I had moved beyond the "You can get it from sitting on a toilet seat" phase. But of course, I was doing a lot more than sitting on toilet seats.

My need to find out what was wrong with me, and how long I had to live, consumed me. I had to see a doctor, but I didn't know what to tell my parents. The admission that I had fallen victim to something so hideous seemed impossible to communicate to them. I had no idea how they would react. Maybe they would ban me from the dinner table or, worse, the hot tub.

I began faking an illness to get my mom to take me to the doctor. A little cough, some aches and pains, a general malaise, until my mother thought I was anemic. After making me take iron supplements for several weeks and still the symptoms persisted, she then became convinced that I had chronic fatigue syndrome. Because she did. At last, she was convinced that I needed a physical.

My pediatrician was suspicious of my visit, but he went through the routine anyhow. I jogged in place, I turned, I coughed, and everything checked out normal.

"What, then," he said, looking over those final moments of my pristine medical chart, "really brings you in here today?"

I looked down at my pale legs pressed against that butcher paper doctors put on their tables, took a deep breath, then broke the grave news to him.

"Dude, I need an AIDS test."

I'd expected his eyes to open in fear, until he'd nod, shake my hand firmly, tell me, "You're a brave young man, son," and perform the test.

Instead, he laughed. And laughed. And laughed.

"What makes you think you need an AIDS test?" he asked once the laughter subsided.

I was offended. Here I was, a sexually active teen and the only person in whom I could confide mocked me. Did he think I wasn't capable of contracting AIDS? Did my teen awkwardness imply virginity? I was lead guitarist of Onyxx, goddam it!

Full of indignation, I pulled down my tightie whities (boxers were an impossibility beneath leather pants) and showed him.

With each day that passed in the three weeks that it took to get the results of an AIDS test back, I became twice as sure as I had been the day before that I had HIV. I couldn't sleep at night and I had no appetite, which seemed to further prove my condition.

In the meantime, my pediatrician had given me a type of brown salve for my "problem," but as of yet, it hadn't gone away, still more evidence, I was sure, of my compromised immune system.

When the results of the test finally did come in, I was about to leave on a trip with my mother and bandmates up to Mammoth Lakes, a resort city a few hundred miles northeast of Los Angeles.

Set in the high Sierra, the area is breathtaking, a Mecca for skiers in the winter and hikers, bikers, and fishermen in the summer. My mom had fond memories of retreating to Mammoth with her father, so she had decided that perhaps a trip into Mother Nature would reestablish some sense of normalcy in her son and his friends. Yet there was no way in hell I was going to enjoy Devil's Postpile or any other of the natural wonders of Mammoth Lakes with matters such as the health of my immune system weighing on my mind.

As I sat in the passenger seat of my mom's Acura and she backed out of the garage, I told her I'd forgotten my toothbrush and had to run back in. Once inside, I headed straight for the phone and called the number my pediatrician had given me to get my test results.

A woman picked up on the other end, and I blurted, "I need my test results!"

"Name please?" She was far too calm, I felt, given the dire circumstances.

An anonymous name was used for tests in those pre-*Philadelphia* days to avoid discrimination should you test positive. Which I surely would.

"Jimi Hendrix."

There was a shuffling of papers. Oh, shit. They had to give a special speech for the HIV positive and she was searching for the piece of paper it was written on. My stomach sunk, until . . .

"Oh, hi, Craig." So much for anonymity. "You're negative."

I almost collapsed to the floor. I was elated—thrilled. I hung up the phone and threw my arms in the air. I was going to live!

My mom came in, annoyed that we weren't yet on the road. "What are you doing in here?"

I threw my arms around her and kissed her on the

cheek. "Nothing. Let's go," I said, and I skipped out to the garage.

As for my "problem," that resolved itself about three hours later, in a restroom in the town of Lone Pine when, at last, the brown salve and my immune system miraculously worked again.

What remained, however, was a sick feeling from the whole experience. My perspective on "Girls, Girls, Girls," the "Unskinny Bop," and "Givin' the Dog a Bone" was irrevocably altered and yet another reality was anchored to my rock 'n' roll fantasy.

The last time I remember Onyxx functioning as a happy unit was in the early part of 1991 when, at last, we laid down a four-song demo at a recording studio in Orange County.

In the nine months since we'd met Barbi, which is the typical period of gestation, we had taken all the necessary steps to go from scoring gigs at clubs that were either closed or empty to selling out shows on The Strip. We had rehearsed, hustled, and gotten media, and the result was a loyal fan base that other bands were pining to tap into by booking shows with us.

We were far from being the biggest band on The Strip, but since Swingin' Thing was heading for Japan (they actually did have a tour planned), Pretty Boy Floyd's album wasn't catching on, and Cry Wolf and another Strip band called Tuff had disappeared to record their albums, the time seemed ripe for Onyxx to attempt an ascent.

We continued to play shows almost every weekend, mostly opening slots at The Roxy, The Whisky, Gazzarri's, and The Troubadour. We had even earned the affection of a young lady who wrote concert reviews for *Screamer* under the nom de plume "Dragon." The Thursday after any of our shows, we'd rush down to the local Tower Records, pick up a *Screamer*, and see what Dragon had to say. Her reviews of Onyxx gigs were always favorable, and they served to increase both our popularity and our delusions.

Yet, in order to land a record contract, we needed to have something more than our "energetic stage show" to present to A&R reps. Had the Capitol Records representative had something to give his bosses so they could hear the magic for themselves, maybe Cry Wolf wouldn't have been signed and Onyxx would be recording our album instead. So we decided to record a demo.

Barbi found a studio near our homes, in, surprisingly, a business park. The owner was also the producer, a quiet black man named Yorman Williams who sat in a glassed-in mixing room at the front of the studio. Far from the four-track mixer I'd set up in the sauna at Tyler's dad's house, Yorman's soundboard was the real deal, with no fewer than sixteen tracks. Yorman was complimentary upon our meeting, claiming he'd heard of Onyxx and was excited to work with us. We told him we were excited, too, and once we handed him his $500 fee, we got to work.

There were separate rooms for each of us, with the largest room housing Kyle's drums. I was relegated to what appeared to be a broom closet far down the hallway, where I set up my equipment and made sure my guitar was in tune.

By this time I had acquired no fewer than nine guitars, some of which I'd purchased and some of which were loaned to me by friends. When you go to a concert and you see a guitarist changing guitars, there are many reasons for this. Different guitars carry different sounds, or sometimes they are tuned differently for specific songs. It's much easier for an axman to simply have an instrument that's already tuned to D, for example, standing by should he need it, rather than trying to retune it in front of 17,000 people.

I, on the other hand, had nine guitars simply because I liked telling people I had nine guitars. Some of them were even quite nice. Yet for reasons lost to history, I brought a cheap Korean Stratocaster knockoff that I'd borrowed from a neighbor for the recording session. I think I had it in my head that this guitar sounded better on tape, but it constantly fell out of tune and actually sounded like an instrument you'd hear at a Chinese restaurant. Yorman told me not to worry about it; he'd make the guitar sound just fine. He had sixteen tracks, for God's sake. He could do anything. By the end of the morning, we had completed the sound check and were ready to record.

Which songs to lay down had been decided the night before at the condo. Typically, a demo is three or four songs long, but we felt we needed four to best display the multifaceted nature of our music. Since the first track was also the first thing any A&R rep would hear, you wanted to lead off with your best song. In our case, it was a no-brainer. "Another Tear" was by far our most popular song, and it would undoubtedly lead to that rep listening to the second song, Sonny's Barbi-inspired "In Your Heart." Acoustic ballads were guaranteed hits and had put more than a few bands, including Extreme, Saigon Kick, and Mr. Big, on the charts.

The final two songs were a bit more contentious, but ultimately we decided on "Living It Up" for track number three. It was our longest song, and it was one that had been a part of our repertoire since our first show. It showcased our instrumentation, which in retrospect was probably something we didn't want to attract attention to. We then decided to close with "Life Behind the Scenes," a straight-up rocker about what it's really like to walk in Onyxx's boots, the world you wouldn't see just by coming to a show or a hotel afterparty or read about in the *Los Angeles Times*.

We all retreated to our separate rooms, connected only through Yorman's wizardry, listening to one another through headphones. It took the entirety of the afternoon to record all four songs, running through each of them countless times. "Living It Up" was particularly challenging because it had several movements and Kyle struggled with the transitions. As the afternoon dragged on and it became clear Kyle wasn't going to get it, Yorman gave Kyle a metronome click in his earphone so that he could keep beat.

This was a moment of great humiliation for Kyle, as it should be for any drummer, but one of satisfaction for Sonny. As the better half of Onyxx's rhythm section,

Sonny was vindicated in his contention that Kyle had no sense of rhythm. It also provided Sonny with a defense anytime Kyle would try to harass him about anything, from the fact that he had to iron his hair straight to the color of his skin. Sonny would simply smile and whisper, "Metronome," and all laughter would be redirected toward Kyle.

Finally, we dubbed in several vocal tracks, both lead and backing, until we realized something that was never revealed in our live set: I couldn't really sing. It wasn't just that I was slightly off key, it was the sound my voice made when I tried to manipulate it. It just sounded wrong, like someone who can't really do a British accent quoting *Monty Python*.

So I sat in the mixing room with Yorman and watched Tyler through a glass panel, his eyes closed, veins bulging through his neck as he dubbed in all the vocal tracks. This is the way Jimmy Paige would have done it, too, giving commentary to Robert Plant. So it was okay.

Despite the fact that Tyler could barely speak, let alone sing, by the time we were done, the demo was complete as the sun went down. Recording was far more exhausting than any show we had ever done. Performing was fun—there was an audience to feed off of. Recording was work and nothing more. No one ever fantasized about being locked in a broom closet all day and playing the same four songs over and over. The idea of recording an entire album, at that moment, sounded like misery.

As we loaded our equipment back into Kyle's van, Yorman mixed all the music together. I still don't really know exactly what he did as far as "mixing," but by the time we were packed up, Yorman called us into his little glass booth to tell us it was complete. The five of us, including Barbi, stood behind him as he cued up the tape and played our music back for us.

1. "Another Tear": A hi-hat counts off, "one, two, three," followed by double bass drum and a crash! The beat kicks in along with the bass line, running through the four-chord structure that is the pulse of the song. Then the guitar solo begins, and it doesn't seem that Yorman fixed the problem of my guitar. It actually sounds as though someone's playing in a broom closet far down the hallway, and it's almost imperceptibly out of tune with the bass . . . But trust me, you can still perceive it. Finally, Tyler's vocals explode, quite literally. It actually sounds like he's in pain, as though someone is plucking, individually, each one of the hairs from his scalp. The song picks up steam as it goes, though, the chorus having a fun sing-along quality to it. All in all, it's a competent debut.

2. "In Your Heart": There is the sound of a quiet storm, rain falling gently on concrete. Then the acoustic guitar comes in, followed by a lead riff. Again, the guitar seems to not be in the same area code as the rest of the instruments. Because of its simplicity, though, this song comes off even better than "Another Tear." There are no drums, for one thing, and the muted quality of the lead guitar complements the creative rain effect and the somber mood of the song. Then, inexplicably, Kyle begins hitting random cymbals. Between choruses, you can actually hear

me shout, "That's so bad." More amazing still is the fact that Yorman hasn't mixed any of that out. Yet the track still manages to feel like it's being sung around a campfire. Although the singer may be on fire. At the end of side one, the demo's not a complete disaster.

3. "Living It Up": Okay, now it's a disaster. Jesus. The guitar down the street opens the song, anticipating the drums and bass. When they arrive, Tyler whispers, "Saaaaa," something he borrowed from Skid Row's Sebastian Bach, who used it to perfection in "18 and Life." The song really revs up about a minute in, which is where you can hear everything that's wrong with it. Put simply, the metronome didn't help. The only thing going for this song is a creative backing vocal track Tyler improvised, but it's not enough to salvage the song. And the worst part is, it goes on for six minutes or so. Fast forward . . .

4. "Life Behind the Scenes": This song isn't bad. It kind of rocks actually. There is an innovative bass line, and it's full of energy. As a listener, perhaps your ears have just adjusted to the sound of the guitar. The problem is, there don't actually seem to be any lyrics. Tyler is just mumbling, although occasionally something is coherent. "But it's not a glamour life/Sometimes it's hard on life." At least I think that's what he says. The chorus is more decipherable: "It's life behind the scenes/That makes the band's dreams/So when times bring you down/Just think of the neon town/Cause it's life behind the scenes." The song also speeds up during the second verse, then slows back down for the bridge and the chorus. It's a bold drummer who can ignore a metronome. My solo sounds more

like someone is retuning the guitar, Tyler's voice begins to crack, but he makes it to the end of the song. The guitar fades out, and the tape pops to an almost submissive end.

As we looked at one another to gauge a reaction (we were teenagers; no one wanted to be first to express an opinion), we simply shrugged. I knew it wasn't really, you know, good, but I also knew I didn't want to go through the process of recording again. Indifference actually seemed to be the dominant emotion. Until we heard sniffling.

Slowly, we all turned to see Barbi, tears streaming down her face. She shook her head, barely able to speak. "It's beautiful," she finally said, and hugged us.

But I wonder if her tears were more a result of an epiphany. As though, somehow, she knew at that moment, or somewhere halfway through track number three, that no matter how hard we tried, no matter what gimmicks or effects we used, none of it could cover up for a very real fact now preserved for posterity.

We just weren't that good.

And it seemed that now that we had the tape to prove it, more realities would invade our fantasy, and things were going to disintegrate quickly.

The fragile peace that existed between Sonny and Kyle was cultivated primarily by Tyler and me. The source of their feud was rehearsal, where Sonny continued to complain about Kyle's nonexistent sense of rhythm, while Kyle countered that Sonny didn't know what the fuck he was talking about. Whenever tensions would flare, Tyler would pull Kyle aside, I'd take Sonny, and both of us would listen to our wards complain about how big a dick the other guys in the band were.

However, matters were irreparably aggravated when, shortly after we had found Sonny intertwined with Barbi in the hotel hot tub, Barbi celebrated her thirty-ninth birthday by moving on to Kyle.

Rather than a quiet dinner with family and friends, Barbi celebrated the last year of her thirties at a party with sixteen-year-old boys at my parents' house—while my parents were out of town. There was plenty of booze involved, of course, and by the end of the night, Kyle and Barbi wound up in my parents' bedroom—in my parents' bed, to be more precise. Unlike the occurrence with Sonny, however, their relationship was consummated.

I know this not only because my mom found Barbi's dainties in her bedroom closet when she and my dad returned from their vacation and not only because Kyle told me about it in great detail (the description of the Cesarean scar was what affected me most at that age; teenage butt rockers don't like to think of the female form as a utilitarian vessel). I know Kyle and Barbi made tender, statutory-rape-law-bending love because Tyler and I listened to it from just outside the door. We passed a bottle of my dad's vodka back and forth, laughing hysterically as we eavesdropped, not really considering what was actually occurring on the other side of that door.

There were the sounds of them whispering, soft kisses, and something like that of a loaded washing machine during the rinse cycle. Barbi also apparently told Kyle that she was in love with him, but that their age difference prevented them from being together. Sounds like the theme of a pretty kick-ass acoustic ballad, doesn't it?

None of this sat very well with Sonny. He held Kyle personally responsible for his heartbreak and lost all faith in the only person in the band in whom he had any remaining faith. If a Loni Anderson impersonator can let you down, where do you turn?

Which brings us to the violent culmination that occurred on March 15, 1991, during the party that Kyle threw at his parents' house in celebration of his seventeenth birthday.

I was away on a ski trip with my parents and was unable to attend said party, but since there were upwards of one hundred people crammed into the Siegel home, I received numerous eyewitness accounts later and was able to piece together a cohesive narrative.

Despite the fact that he was barely speaking to Kyle at this point, Sonny curiously did attend, pulling in front of Kyle's house in his raised Toyota 4x4 with only the intent of saying happy birthday and being on his way. What Sonny didn't know was that Kyle had been drinking Gran Marnier (and possibly ingesting other substances) for the past several hours and was furious about rumors that Sonny had been critical of his abilities as a drummer. I don't know why Kyle was suddenly upset about this. Sonny, Tyler, and I gave Kyle shit about his lack of rhythm almost daily to his face. All the same, when he heard that Sonny had shown up, Kyle wobbled out to confront him.

The fight began with the usual exchange of words that precedes these sorts of things: "You talkin' shit?" "I heard you been talkin' shit." "Why you talkin' shit?" That kind of thing.

Then, before Sonny could react, Kyle threw a right cross to his nose, and Sonny's face exploded with blood. The entire party watched as Sonny threw Kyle (who was too drunk to stand) to the asphalt and pinned him there. Sonny never threw a punch, and after a moment, he got off of Kyle and told him that was it—he was done with him . . .

. . . And Onyxx.

Q: At what point does a fantasy become a cliché?

A: Whenever it fits into the structural pattern of any Hollywood biopic or, more commonly, any episode of VH1's *Behind the Music.*

As we all know from watching the "Poison" installment of that show, their band disbanded following a cocaine-fueled fistfight between frontman Bret Michaels and guitarist C. C. Deville backstage at the 1991 MTV Video Music Awards. The fight was a result of Deville's cheeky behavior on stage, as, during a performance of "Unskinny Bop," he first played without his guitar plugged in, then played the wrong song. Michaels called bullshit and the fight was on.

Indeed, the Hair Metal fistfight is as much a staple of the genre as the guitar solo. Sebastian Bach of Skid Row seemed to be constantly punching someone, usually an audience member, as was Axl Rose, who challenged virtually every magazine editor he'd ever known to "Get in the Ring" on *Use Your Illusion II*. I don't know where Axl's pugilistic tendencies came from, but perhaps the most famous of his feuds was with Mötley Crüe frontman Vince Neil, who traded barbs with Axl in the press for years about actually scheduling a sanctioned bout. Unfortunately, irrelevance stepped in and called the dispute a draw.

Granted, Kyle and Sonny's Gran Marnier/Barbi-inspired fistfight at a suburban house party wasn't quite as glamorous as other butt rock grudges, and Onyxx hadn't yet accomplished many of the other feats that a band like Poison had (multiplatinum record sales, millions of dollars in the bank, a sex tape with Pamela Anderson, etc.), yet the effect was much the same. By the time I got home from my family vacation on Sunday, the band was in crisis mode and an emergency meeting was called up at the condo.

Sonny still wanted to quit the band, but Barbi urged him to reconsider. She had booked us into an important showcase at The Roxy in April, and she claimed to have A&R reps from five different record companies confirmed to attend. She asked if we could keep it together for just this show.

Sonny and Kyle couldn't even glance at each other. After a long silence, Kyle looked up at Sonny and apologized for punching him in the face. Sonny muttered a disingenuous kind of forgiveness, they hugged, and it appeared the show would go on.

A record company showcase was, I think, the only thing that could have kept Onyxx intact at that point. Yet it's also important to note that none of us had any real reason to believe Barbi's promises that A&R reps would be at the gig. After all, Barbi also once told me that Bret Michaels called her from his airplane to tell her that he had written the song "Something to Believe In" for her. I was skeptical of this, particularly since it was well known that Michaels had written the song for his deceased body-guard and best friend. Yet I was ecstatic about the possibility that five record company reps were coming to my show because I profoundly wanted to believe there were. We all did. This is what we had been working toward for the past quarter of our lives. We would do the show, get multiple offers, and then everything would be fine.

This is what we believed in—what we had to believe in. And if you want to get a sense of how powerful the rock 'n' roll fantasy is, you should know this:

I still believe.

16

Livin' on
a Prayer

I hate to sound cynical (I'm from Orange County, after all, where cynicism has actually been banned in several municipalities), but it's almost always a bad idea to have expectations. I don't mean that people should live without hope, but to expect something implies a sense of entitlement, which inevitably leads to disappointment. To hope that you're going to win the lottery, for example, is amusement. To expect to win the lottery suggests a psychological imbalance. The same logic, I would argue, applies to the rock 'n' roll fantasy.

Yet no one had higher expectations than I going into our showcase at The Roxy in April of 1991. We had paid our dues, I reasoned, and at least one of the record company reps coming to the show would want to sign us. There would probably be a bidding war amongst several of them, in fact, and Onyxx would land a massive record contract. Our album would go on to sell in the tens of millions, we'd be asked to play at the American Music Awards (where'd I'd finally meet Eddie Van Halen backstage), and I'd get to make a heartfelt speech at the Grammys thanking my parents for all their support. The following week, *Rolling Stone* would carry me on its cover with the headline "The Soul Just Happened, Rocker Says."

The final and most severe symptom of the rock star fantasy, apparently, is delusions of grandeur.

What was more interesting was that these delusions spread to those who surrounded us. Barbi, her daughters, some of our fans, and groupies in particular were all inflating our expectations as the show approached. We were gonna get signed, they all told us. We just had to do what we'd been doing, and it would happen.

The only people around us immune to such expectations in the weeks leading up to the showcase were our roadies. The roadie, particularly the club circuit roadie, is a far more mystifying rock star archetype than the groupie simply because he or she doesn't seem to get anything out of the relationship.

Groupies inspire rock stars, but roadies facilitate them. Groupies party with rock stars, but roadies attend and/or bounce rock star parties, often making beer runs. Groupies make love to rock stars, but roadies get screwed by them.

Roadies exist strictly to move equipment, pick girls out of the crowd for the band, and ensure that unwanted people can't get to the band. There could hardly be rock stardom without roadies, as they do everything to make the rock star look and sound like a rock star. Yet they get nothing material in return.

The purest love of music is how they justify their existences. From their perspective, they get a free pass to hear and see live rock, and that's all they need. They are sonic junkies, and to get their fix, they will lug amplifiers up mountains or set up drum kits underwater, so long as they get to listen once everything is in place. They are far more dedicated fans than groupies, bless their hearts, could ever be.

Onyxx's roadies had always been friends of ours, Dan Russo and Sam Welti, both of whom I had known since the G.A.T.E. days. In addition to being huge music fans, they were guys we liked to hang out with. There was nothing ever subservient about their roles, and it's not like we paid them anything; they just got a kick out of seeing their friends act like rock stars.

As our appearances on The Strip occurred with more frequency, however, it became harder for them to always be there. They weren't completely consumed by the fantasy as we were, and Sam in particular had obligations at home to attend to. Specifically, he was a Mormon, on track to be valedictorian of his seminary, and there were evenings when his study of the Angel Moroni took precedence over my need to have someone tune all nine of my guitars.

Russo, on the other hand, was frequently placed on restriction by his parents for various transgressions: smoking, drinking, staying out all night—things that were usually a result of spending too much time with Onyxx.

As it turned out, neither of them would be available to roadie for our showcase at The Roxy, despite our description as to the significance of said show. Nor could we set up our own equipment for a record company showcase; we had to look professional. Fortunately, there were a couple other guys who had been coming to our shows regularly who told us to give them a call if we ever needed a hand.

Pete and Tony were seniors at a high school in Brea, yet another suburb about twenty miles northwest of Anaheim Hills. They went together like Guns went along with Roses, and I don't remember ever seeing them apart. They had roadied for a few other bands on The Strip, and when we called them to request their services, I think one of them responded with an enthusiastic "Fuck yeah, dude."

Both were thin and pale, always wearing skin-tight black jeans and one concert T-shirt or another. They were distinguished from each other by their hair: Tony had a well-kempt dark coif, something like a latter-day Chris Cornell, while Pete paid little attention to a poofy blond Afro that resembled that of *Tommy*-era Roger Daltrey.

They came by the rehearsal studio a few times before the gig so they could see how everything worked. After we showed them, we assumed they'd be on their way, but they would then stay for the entire rehearsal, sitting in a corner and banging their heads as though to say, "Yes, yes, you guys rock!" ad infinitum.

For Pete and Tony, indeed for any roadie, rock, even bad teenager butt rock, was transcendent. The setting was irrelevant. This duo was just as happy sitting on the floor of our studio, listening with their eyes closed, as they would be at The Roxy, The Coliseum, or anyplace else, listening to anyone else. They simply loved to rock, and there is hardly a religion in the world more pure, more inspiring.

In return, they expected nothing. The night of the showcase, after sound check, we took Pete and Tony to Carney's, an old train car on Sunset that had been converted into a hot dog stand. For their services, we bought them a hot dog and a soda, and I thought they were going to weep with gratitude. "You guys," they told us breathlessly, "are the coolest fucking band on The Strip. We're gonna tell everyone."

They were rock 'n' roll Buddhists, having eliminated all expectation or desire from their lives through the power of head banging meditation. In many ways, I envied their devotion, their single-minded dedication to something so easily dismissed by countless others.

Unfortunately, on the night of the showcase, April 26, 1991, we discovered that Pete and Tony weren't entirely adept at setting up our equipment.

The difference between a regular show and a showcase is that a show will have multiple bands performing over the course of an evening. A showcase is a presentation of one band, in this case, Onyxx, specifically for record companies. For us, it was really the first time we were standing on our own.

As usual, we'd done everything to promote the show. In addition to passing out fliers on The Strip, we continued to run our ad in *Screamer* with the Roxy show date. Despite the fact that three members of the band were seventeen by this time, the ad still carried the "They're only 16!" exploding bubble in the corner. We believed sixteen to be infinitely more impressive than seventeen.

We were also more hardcore about promoting the show at school than we had been in years, explaining to our classmates the significance of this showcase. We wanted these record company reps to witness the frenzy that was an Onyxx show, even if some of our fans might also be described as "lab partners."

It wasn't too big a surprise, then, when Barbi came backstage at The Roxy with her trademark semi-psychotic smile and told us the club was filled to capacity. Of course it was, we thought. We expected as much.

Everyone we had ever come in contact with, it seemed, was there. The girls who had come to see Devolution when we first started playing shows in the playroom, Shannon's friends (although not Shannon), girls whose birthday parties we had rocked, the woman who claimed to be having Kyle's child, Baby, and even the Great White groupies were all there.

As, of course, were all five A&R reps from various record companies. At no point did I ever meet any of these

A&R reps, but according to Barbi, Arista, Warner Brothers, Chrysalis, Atlantic, and the guy from Capitol Records who had seen us once before had all taken seats in various corners of The Roxy Theater. Again, this didn't surprise any of us; we fully expected it. Which is why we had done nothing but rehearse since Kyle had punched Sonny a few weeks before.

Their truce was tenuous, and they maintained it simply by not talking to each other. It wasn't necessarily tense during rehearsals, but Sonny seemed disconnected, almost as though he was just doing us a favor by being there. Still, by the night of the show, we had our set down fairly tight, and we had planned a few surprises, particularly for the encore, that were sure to dazzle fan and industry folk alike. We were much more prepared than we had been two and a half years before for our first show at Chexx. "If that record company rep could see us now," we all mused.

As the Roxy's house lights went down, Barbi hugged us and told us all to have a great show. We weren't nervous—just eager to get started. Between the time that we'd done sound check and provided the Great Gift of the Hot Dog for our roadie congregation, an interminable number of hours seemed to have passed, and we were tired of sitting around. We were like thoroughbreds just before the Kentucky Derby, chomping at the bit.

As Barbi left us, our intro music faded up over the PA. I had insisted on the climactic movement from Beethoven's Ninth and had worked out a very elaborate finger-tapping guitar solo for the segment popularly known as "Ode to

Joy." It was an ambitious choice, to be sure, but this was hardly the time to play it safe.

Sonny and I were now using wireless devices on both our guitars, meaning we weren't plugged directly into our amplifiers by any cables. This allowed us the freedom to move about the stage unrestricted. It also permitted me to screw around on my guitar from backstage before the show started—to whet the appetite of the crowd before we came on. Whenever an audience hears a live instrument after they've been waiting for what surely felt like hours, cheers are always aroused.

My plan was, when "Ode to Joy" came on, I would covertly shred up my guitar solo from backstage, and just as it ended, the sound guy would kill the intro music, I'd rip into the opening riff of "Rise High," the lights would come up, and we'd explode on to the stage.

"O Freunde, nicht diese tone!" the fat man howled through the darkness of The Roxy Theater, literally translated as, "Oh, shit, not this song!" The horns and flutes flirted with the melody, then backed off, a lone oboe carrying the rhythm, the chorus ready to explode. And then the rapid crescendo until BOOM! All the pieces united: horns, strings, woodwinds, percussion, and a chorus of fat Germans in one of the most inspired melodies ever written.

The A&R reps would be stunned by my versatility and the insight with which we conducted our shows. This was not the dumbed-down rump rock of Pretty Boy Floyd. This was classically inspired, literate Hair Metal, and it was sure to be added to the canon of great musical conquest. I turned up the volume knob on my guitar to take my place among the chorus, and plucked away at my solo . . .

. . . Only to find that no sound was coming out of my amplifier.

I ran out of the dressing room and down the narrow hallway of stairs to the curtain leading to the stage. I poked my head out to see—indeed, the place was packed. People looked around at one another, confused by the unexpected choice of music. My guitar solo was meant to explain it, but having missed my chance, the music just carried on without purpose. And it's a twenty-minute movement. I spotted Tony the roadie at the foot of the stage and waved him over. He rushed to my side.

"There's nothing coming out of my amp!"

He gave me a thumbs-up, then scurried off to check all my cables and my effects pedals, all of which appeared to be functioning normally. Again he gave me a thumbs-up from where my amp stood on stage, again I hit a chord on my guitar, and again I got nothing.

The rest of the band came down the stairs and crowded behind me.

"What's going on?"

"I have no volume!"

"Wwwwwwhat the fffffuck's wrong?"

"I don't know!"

"Well fix it!"

The last thing I wanted to do was expose myself to the audience. That completely killed the air of mystery and anticipation. But I also didn't think I could hide behind that curtain all night and wait for my guitar to miraculously start working. I had to fix it.

Reluctantly, I ran out on stage to have a look for myself, avoiding the gaze of the girls pressed up against the front of the stage. I turned off my amp and disconnected everything—while Beethoven's Ninth continued to play. When I reconnected, my amp was still useless. I began to sweat, not with the traditional droplets coming down from the brow, but more of an upwelling through every pore in my body, like a backed-up shower drain. My stomach turned as I could feel the eyes of the entire club on me. I knew that utter panic was setting in. The Beethoven wasn't helping.

As a last resort, I disconnected my wireless and all my effects pedals and plugged my guitar directly into my amp. I stood back, took a swipe at my guitar, and then there was rock. It would be stripped down, unaffected rock, which wasn't really our thing, but it had worked at Spanky's. Certainly, it was better than the silence I had been getting up to that point.

I looked up and nodded at my bandmates, who nodded back. I stood and faced the audience while Kyle climbed in behind his drum kit. Once he was situated, I gestured for the sound guy to kill the Beethoven, and once it was gone, I hit the opening riff of "Rise High." Without my effects the song sounded a little weak, but the lights exploded, Tyler leapt off the drum riser, and a cheer went up from the crowd.

While my mobility was limited by the cable, and the guitar didn't sound exactly the way I wanted it to, the showcase at The Roxy was one of the best shows in the history of Onyxx. I think we were as tight as we ever sounded: Tyler's voice was strong and on key, and Kyle was somehow miraculously on beat throughout. Or so it seems to me now.

And maybe it was the pent-up energy from sitting around for so long, but our stage presence was full of energy that night. Kyle spun his sticks and threw them out into the audience after a particularly kick-ass song. I strutted to the front of the stage during solos, put my boot up on the speaker cabinet, pointed to girls, and threw guitar picks out to them. I might have even winked. Tyler put me in a headlock, kneeled down and sang to the front row, and pointed the microphone out to the audience to let them sing along, just like Bon Jovi would.

In return, the audience was frenzied, and not just because we told them to be. It was genuinely a solid show, and as we finished "Another Tear," our final song, we disappeared backstage so that the crowd could beg for the surprises we'd planned for our encore.

We allowed the applause to simmer for a few minutes, not only for our own satisfaction, but also for the benefit of the A&R reps.

"Did you see any of them out there?"

"I did. At a table up on the right."

"How do you know it's an A&R guy?"

"He's by himself."

We high-fived, pulled one another in for hugs, and then took to the stage again to even more applause.

The first surprise we had for our fans was that, rather

than taking up our normal instruments, we all took different positions. Sonny took my guitar, Kyle took Sonny's bass, and I took the microphone from Tyler, who got behind the drum kit. Once we were set, I looked out over the crowd to give them their second surprise.

"Anybody here ever heard of Baron Von Rock?" I screamed.

The audience cheered to confirm they had, as BVR's Mikey and Markey came out of the audience and onto the stage. This had been planned for weeks, of course, but it seemed entirely improvised, I'm sure.

Since the shows we had done with BVR and Swingin' Thing, we had become pretty good friends with Mikey and Markey. I wasn't going to invite them over for pool volleyball at my folks' house or anything, but whenever we'd see each other on The Strip, we'd perform complicated handshakes, give one another one-armed hugs and slaps on the back—that sort of thing.

As the crowd cheered for their other favorite up-and-coming act on The Strip, I tried to quiet them down for the final surprise of the evening.

"Hold up a second," I said, "this is important," and the crowd began to settle down, perhaps a little nervous, as though more of Beethoven's Ninth might be played. "Guys, seriously, shut up. Tyler has something important he needs to say." This, too, had been planned, but the audience seemed actually concerned and The Roxy was filled with a grave quiet.

I walked back to the drum riser and held the microphone out for Tyler. He took a deep breath, the stage lights beating down on him, blue and red beads of sweat falling from the tip of his nose. He held up the drum sticks and clicked them together as he counted off, "One, two, three, four!"

We burst into The Ramones's "Blitzkrieg Bop," and the crowd went insane.

I jumped around the stage, while Mikey and Markey stood spread-legged behind the back-up mics, just like Joey Ramone would have. I hopped onto Markey's back and he piggy-backed me around the stage while I continued to sing. I was in control of the audience and the stage, and the girls in the front row looked up at me with awe. It was exactly as the seven-year-old me had envisioned it, with Mikey and Markey filling in for Olivia Newton John and Donna Summer.

Goddam it, I was a rock star.

At the end of the song, I collapsed on the stage while Baron Von Rock and the rest of Onyxx dog-piled on top of me. The roar of the crowd was as deafening as several hundred people possibly can be. Once the lights went down, we strutted off the stage, jumping on one another's backs as we headed back up the stairwell to our dressing room, triumphant and infinitely confident. If ever a record company was going to sign Onyxx, it was that night.

Barbi came backstage to tell us we'd done it. Arista was very interested, and she was going to have some drinks with the A&R rep to talk things over.

"Should we meet him?"

"No, you guys go celebrate. You've earned it."

We didn't need to meet him. We'd meet him when we

signed the deal. We went back to the Travelodge and partied as though we already had a mega-contract.

I remember very little about the celebration that night, except for that blindly ecstatic state that only youth can submit to when expectations haven't been tempered by reality. It seemed wonderful that a woman in her twenties brought her own guitar and insisted on singing "Babe I'm Gonna Leave You," by Zeppelin really, really loud. We all sang along with her, eyes closed, arms dangling over one another's shoulders, plastic cups in the air, champagne spilling over the sides and running down our hands. The fact that Kyle was having sex with a different woman while Tyler and I slapped his ass in encouragement seemed enchanting. It was the celebration we all expected it to be—what we deserved.

But the thing I remember most was this:

Sonny was nowhere to be found.

Don't Cry

(alt. lyrics)

Onyxxx . . . our last gasp.

Dear Onyxx suporters [*sic*]

We would like to take this time to tell you how sorry we are for the incident of the cancelation [*sic*] of our last show and as fans you have the right to know what exactly is going on. A couple of months ago our bassist felt the urge that the flame for him was fading so ever since he has been hanging from a string. Our management also has had similar feelings for that flame, but not in us but being in a band really takes a lot out of a person. So with all of these problems at one time we felt that a cancellation of the show was in order. But our proposition for all of your troubles is we intend to keep what you have given us and mail out these free tickets for the June 15, Yes this show is is [*sic*] our debue [*sic*] at support slot as well as the debut of our new bassist. The show starts at 10:00 and it takes place at Gazzaris [*sic*] with the almighty headlingner [*sic*] BARON VON ROCK PLUS get this anymore tickets that are bought for this show if you send me back this letter is only 5 dollars so tell your friends and thanks for everything if you only knew how much you guys mean to us.

Sincerely
ONYXX

Tyler's letter was composed in May of 1991 explaining to Onyxx fans everywhere why we'd had to cancel our follow-up show to the showcase at The Roxy. Since it's apparent to me now that the reason Tyler never wrote down his lyrics may have been a functional illiteracy, allow me to translate. There are, essentially, three points to the letter.

The first is that, the day after the showcase, Sonny came by my house and broke the news to me: He was done with Onyxx, only this time he meant it. Where he had always been an outsider trying to fit in, he now carried with him a profound indifference he previously hadn't possessed.

I thought his timing couldn't have been worse. We were on the verge of getting signed, I told him. It was everything we'd ever wanted. But he said it wasn't what he wanted anymore. Senior year was coming up and he needed to focus on going to college. He was committed to getting admitted to Berkeley, and he needed to get serious about it. Onyxx was taking up too much of his time, and playing bass in a Hair Metal band wasn't what he wanted to do for the rest of his life, anyway.

While I always believed his collegiate aspirations were part of his decision, the real reason, it turns out, was much simpler.

"I didn't like you guys," he tells me today. "I mean, I guess part of it's that we weren't good, but mostly I just thought you guys were kind of tools and I didn't want to hang out with you anymore."

Fair enough. But this was by no means enough to derail my fantasy.

At an emergency meeting up at the condo, Barbi told us we had more problems. An offer never came in from Arista—or any other record label. In the fantasy version of this story, the one I've told for years at cocktail parties and weddings, the A&R reps were frightened off by Onyxx's instability, tendency toward chaos, or something along those lines.

But, part of my recovery process is trying to look at what really happened. In all probability, if any A&R reps were at our showcase at all, they popped our demo into the tape decks of their Saabs on their way home and made it through two and a half songs before chucking the tape out the window and speeding away as its guts scattered across the asphalt.

To make matters worse, in the Onyxx P.O. box, we received yet more cease and desist papers from that law firm in London in regard to the use of the name Onyxx. (In addition to hip-hop Onyx, I have come to learn that there was a female butt rock band called Onyxx based out of Austin, Texas.) Not only did we need a new bassist, we needed, once again, a new name.

This seemed horribly unfair to me. We'd spent the past year building up our name and reputation around The Strip, and now we were going to lose all that cachet.

Since we had no choice in the matter, we set about coming up with a new name. I went for something that might reflect the image and marketability of the band and suggested the name Playground. Tyler and Kyle hated it. They thought it sounded too young, and Kyle rebutted with the name Whoreable.

Unable to come to an agreement, we decided to keep the one we already had, but just alter the spelling a little. Again.

Which is how we became Onyxxx.

As for finding a replacement for Sonny, we didn't conduct a nationwide talent search or even create a reality show out of auditioning bassists. In fact, we didn't hold auditions at all. Instead, we decided to take on Pete, our bushy-haired, incompetent roadie. If you thought he was excited about the hot dog at Carney's . . .

He leapt around during rehearsals, slapping at the bass like a chimpanzee, and after every song, he would say something to the effect of, "That was fucking solid, man." When we would bring him out to parties, he would hold long conversations with potential fans in which he would compare and contrast the size of his phallus in its flaccid and erect states.

More irritating, Kyle and Tyler continued the escalation of their drug use. Since I had no desire to masturbate until I bled, or retile my parents' entire backyard, I never touched the stuff and spent more and more time away from Kyle and Tyler, attempting to write classical guitar compositions (they were never "songs"). This was a mostly solitary pursuit, and one that drew the ire of both Tyler and Kyle. With Sonny gone, it became apparent that the new outsider was I.

Even Barbi, our beacon of principles, didn't seem to care for the direction Onyxxx had taken, what with her favorite songwriter out of the band and the even more awkward name. Which brings us to the second point of Tyler's letter to our fans.

When Barbi showed up to rehearsal one afternoon, which she almost never did, I knew something was afoot. Being the optimist that I am, I assumed she'd come to tell us one of the record labels had changed their minds, having listened to our demo, and now wanted to sign Onyxxx to a multialbum deal.

Instead, she took a deep breath and said, "I'm resigning as manager of Onyxxx." She said this gravely, in much the same way I had seen videos of Nixon's resignation in government class. Barbi believed she may have been the source of some tension in the band and that Onyxxx might be better off without her. Where she would have come up with such an idea is beyond me, yet I do know it's unlikely Onyxxx would have achieved any of the glory it had without her.

She then walked up to me, standing inches from my face, and began to cry. "I'm especially sorry for you, Craig." I thought I might cry, too. "I know this was always your dream, and I hope you continue to pursue it." She hugged me, and it was a little like the scene in *Wizard of Oz* when Dorothy is saying good-bye to all her friends, and I was the scarecrow. I was taken aback by her sincerity as well as the apparent transparence of my sickness.

Still, Onyxxx endured. We replaced Barbi with James McFarlane, the manager at our rehearsal studio. With all the changes we'd undergone in the course of a few weeks, his advice was to consider seriously taking our music in a different direction, too. This was, he assured us, a chance to reinvent ourselves. In addition to my newfound appreciation for Jane's Addiction, he managed to get me obsessed with Nine Inch Nails's *Pretty Hate Machine*, but none of it had any effect on the music Onyxxx was playing. We were disciples of the Hollywood Hair Metal scene, and we weren't likely to suddenly convert.

James's other piece of advice was to hold off on booking any new shows until we could get our sound tight, which brings us to the third and final point of Tyler's letter: We had to cancel the show we had booked at Gazzarri's while we regrouped.

Rather than eating the pay-to-play fee and returning money to anyone who had bought tickets, we kept it and promised "free" tickets to our next show. This may have been an error of both business and tact.

As with our sound, we assured James we knew what we were doing, so we booked a show with Baron Von Rock on Saturday, June 15, one day after I completed my junior year of high school.

With the band at least functioning once again, Tyler wrote his ode to sincerity to try to get fans to our show. With prose like his, how could it fail?

The worst sound you can hear after finishing a song in a club is not booing or even a heartfelt "faggot!" The worst sound you can hear after finishing a song is coughing.

Gazzarri's was empty on June 15, save a few bartenders who apparently had the croup. I don't even remember if Baron Von Rock bothered to show up.

Onyxxx sounded as awful as the name looks. Tyler's voice cracked throughout, Kyle's rhythm was again non-existent, Pete's bass playing was overwhelming, and I seemed to have forgotten how to play guitar. The hole left by Sonny couldn't be filled, although things didn't really implode until about halfway through the set.

James walked in. He was amazed at the emptiness of the club and winced at the sound of the band. At that point, I remember Tyler having something like a breakdown.

He sat down on the drum riser, sweating and out of breath, and started talking directly to James through the microphone.

"Oh, James. Thank God you're here."

James looked around, self-conscious, brought his finger to his lips, telling Tyler to shut up.

"You were right," Tyler went on, his confession still carrying the house reverb. "We weren't ready. We shouldn't have done this show. I'm sorry." I could hear chuckles in the back. "We shouldn't have done it."

Having at long last lost what remained of my dignity, I simply shook my head, unplugged my guitar, and walked off the stage.

Stranger still was the feeling on The Strip in June of 1991. The sidewalks weren't crowded with people asking for autographs, bands weren't handing out fliers, and no one was taking pictures. The whole scene seemed to have died sometime between our showcase in April and June 15. It felt as though the members of Onyxxx were the last ones at a house party, and no one had told us that the festivities had moved to someone else's house about 1,500 miles up the coast to Seattle.

We were still two months away from the Romulus and Remus of grunge, Pearl Jam's *Ten* and Nirvana's *Nevermind*, so it's absurd for salty old butt rockers to claim that grunge is what did the Hollywood scene in. By the summer of 1991, the mood of society had changed. People were no longer looking for "Nothing But a Good Time." They were looking for jobs. The last thing college kids with little hope for gainful employment wanted to see was a group of guys with teased hair, leather vests, and neon guitars rolling around on a stage and giving one another noogies.

What killed Glam Metal were the excesses of Glam Metal itself. Fat men with cocaine-bloated hearts and ratty hair killed Glam Metal. Mediocre musicianship and vapid lyrical content killed Glam Metal. I mean, if you're

going to write a song about having sex with fat girls—
and you shouldn't, by the way, but if you absolutely
must—and the best witticism you can come up with is
"Unskinny Bop," then it may be time to rethink the
whole thing. Brush fires have more subtlety. Glam Metal
had become like a joke that had been taken one step too
far, one beat too long, and the crowd just stopped laughing. It was that quick. I was just lucky enough to be up on
stage at the precise moment the laughter turned to disgust.

In the ensuing weeks, the pages of *Screamer* took on a
whole new look. Many of the bands I had seen trolling
around The Strip the last few years had undergone
makeovers. The hair was still there, for the most part, but
it was flatter and stringier, and in place of any kind of
makeup was the goatee. The wardrobes, too, had been
suddenly altered, and I began to see much more of the
corduroy and flannel that I had seen on Alice in Chains
and Soundgarden.

Indeed, the butt rockers of the Sunset Strip appeared to
have shed any evidence of having ever worn leather pants.

The Monday after our Gazzarri's abomination, we
told Pete he was out of the band. We then brought in our
old roadie and friend Russo. He knew all our songs, and
he was really into meth, too. Once again, the sound just
wasn't what I thought it had been, and about two songs
into our set at rehearsal, sometime in the hazy summer of
1991, I just stopped playing.

"Does anyone actually want to be in this band anymore?" I asked.

They all looked around at one another, and no one answered. Kyle shrugged, gave me a smug smirk.

"Fuck it," I said, unplugging my guitar. "Let's just stop, then." They all froze and continued to stare at me. "This hasn't been fun in a long time. I don't want to do it anymore."

"Me neither," Tyler said, and unplugged his microphone.

Kyle sat behind his kit, looking back from Tyler to me, his tongue paralyzed in his mouth.

"Sssssso that's it?"

I rolled up my cables and unplugged the rest of my gear. "Yup."

"Ssss . . ." He rolled his eyes, frustrated. "Sssseriously? We're done? The band's breaking up?"

"Yes," I said. "We're done."

Tyler had already left the room, but Kyle didn't budge. He just stared at me as I hoisted my amp up and carried it out to my car.

After I'd dropped my equipment in my car, I went back inside Bands West to say good-bye to James. We hugged, promised to keep in touch, and naturally never did.

As I drove away, there was no overwhelming sense of finality or sadness, but more of liberation. It will always be my contention that Onyxxx broke up when Sonny left the band, and me walking out of that rehearsal studio was an inevitable formality.

Onyxxx, no matter how many X's we gave ourselves, was never destined for more than what we were. And what we were was not very good. At our best, Onyxxx was a decent Sunset Strip band that could have come into being only at that exact time and in that exact place.

Onyxxx wasn't a band you'd hear on the radio (although "Another Tear" was played on KNAC's local hour once or twice) or in a stadium, yet we managed to have all the problems of a band that was.

In the months—even years—after I walked out of that studio, I would often think that Onyxxx could have made it, writing and rewriting in my head the power ballad sung by every person sick with the fantasy: "If only."

If only just a few things had played out differently. If only we'd gotten a few breaks to go our way. If only we hadn't had a name that had to be changed every six months or a manager who had a blatant disregard for statutory rape laws. If only we'd been nicer to Sonny and made him feel more a part of the band. If only I could have afforded the right effects for my guitar to make it sound better, or if only Kyle had been able to buy more cymbals for his kit. If only Kyle and Tyler hadn't fallen into the world of drugs. If only I hadn't slept with that one girl on New Year's Eve who I'm pretty sure gave me that STD. If only we'd had a singer who could really sing—or at least scream in key. If only we'd had a drummer who could keep beat. If only we'd spent a little more time on that demo—if only we'd had different songs to put on it. If only I'd set out in pursuit of musical greatness rather than an image, a pose, and a contingency of my peers to bear witness. If only I'd had the perseverance to become what the seven-year-old me had aspired to, that phenom who, in my head, dazzled the likes of Olivia Newton John and Donna Summer and their crowds of thousands. If only.

But, come on, let's be realistic.

Use Your Illusion

When I was twenty-six, I found myself on a date at a restaurant in West Hollywood, a few miles east of the Sunset Strip. I was with a woman who, as it turned out, had recently broken up with her boyfriend of several years who, as it turned out, was Taylor Hawkins who, as it turned out, had recently become drummer for the Foo Fighters.

I had seen the Foos live several times and knew this drummer well. He kicks ass, as any drummer who plays behind one of the most primal drummers since Keith Moon must, and I told her so. Plus, I've always thought, Mr. Hawkins is quite the looker. Why on earth would she have broken up with someone as cool as that only to now be on a date with a wannabe writer? She then told me of the photos she had seen of her ex-boyfriend with a certain actress in *Star* or *Us Weekly* or one of those "magazines."

"Wow," I said, with all the sensitivity of the steamed artichoke we were sharing. "So did you get to meet Dave Grohl?"

She paused. "Yeah. He's really cool."

I spent the rest of the evening grilling her about Mr. Grohl and his feud with Courtney Love and fantasizing about the tangential relationship between this woman sitting across from me and Kurt Cobain. Maybe, I thought, if things worked out, I could jam with her ex-boyfriend, we could start a band, and, well, you know the rest.

She politely, although somewhat curtly, answered all of my queries, as though telling me about her semifamous ex-boyfriend and the life she used to live with him were precisely the topics she wanted to cover on a date. But at the end of the night, when I dropped her off and she quickly leapt out of my car without so much as a hug, it occurred to me that this woman had no idea of the rock star I was—or had almost been.

Gone were any markings of my membership in that tribe, having never received any tattoos (I was too frightened of the irrevocability of such action) and having lopped off my hair three years prior while under the influence of several pints in Manchester, England. She didn't see her date that evening as a rocker who had sold out shows in the clubs that still stood only a few blocks away from that restaurant, but as a short-haired, bespectacled *fan*. Hell, with all my idiotic questions, she probably thought I was some kind of groupie.

What was more disturbing, though, was that this was my concern rather than the fact that I had just blown any shot I might have had with a beautiful, intelligent woman.

As I drove home, listening to *Thirteen Tales from Urban*

Bohemia, making myself feel better by fantasizing that I was a Dandy Warhol on some stage somewhere, probably Portland, where plenty of ladies would kill to have dinner with me, I suddenly came to a very important realization:

I needed help.

How, I wondered, had this happened to me?

A few weeks after Onyxxx broke up, I was contacted by another Strip band and asked to replace their guitarist. Glam Metal groups were falling apart in huge leather clumps in 1991, but these guys were going to try to fight through it. There was absolutely no hesitation in my rejection of their offer, and I returned to playing my guitar, alone, in my bedroom, dreaming of playing before a crowd of adoring fans. The fantasy, it seemed to me, is much more appealing than the reality.

My last official live performance occurred in the spring of 1992 for the Carmen Dragon Chapter of the South Coast Repertory of Music, which consisted of my mom and five of her friends sitting on our dining room chairs in our living room. It was a classical performance of Bach, Haydn, all those cats. The ladies were very impressed with my virtuosity, although I did not get laid after the show and did not autograph a single breast.

Later that fall, in between listening to the *Use Your Illusion* albums incessantly and rejecting anything that came from Seattle as "simplistic," it suddenly occurred to me that I might need to do things like take the SATs and apply to college. I made a last-minute push to get into the University of Southern California's Film Scoring program—only to be rejected. I realized that USC's dismissal of my application had less to do with my timeliness and more to do with my musical ineptitude.

It's not that I was that bad as much as it was that I wasn't that good. It was a realization that had been creeping up on me for some time, from studying Hendrix's solo on "Red House," which I'd simply never be able to play, to seeing bands that were far more talented than I performing in the same clubs I had, yet were still only marginally successful, like Saigon Kick (at The Roxy) or Salty Dog (at The Whisky).

It seemed to me then that it might be time to let go of my rock 'n' roll fantasy. I thought I'd done a pretty good job of it, too, until that date in West Hollywood. Recovery, as it turns out, is a work in progress.

The thing is, the rock 'n' roll fantasy isn't something you really ever get over. This is why the Rolling Stones continue to tour (I'm sure the $500 million on the 2006 tour didn't hurt, either) and why grown men and women pay close to $10,000 for five days at Rock 'N' Roll Fantasy Camp.

To be a rock star, you see, is to achieve the pinnacle of celebrity. Not in the colloquial sense of someone who is simply well known, but in the sense that someone is celebrated with reverence.

Recently, some friends were telling me of their trip to Rome, where they were lucky enough to witness an appearance by the pope.

"It was unbelievable," they told me. "Like seeing a rock star."

Consider that. The patriarch of one of the globe's major religions, a mortal some believe to be in close communication with the divine, is *like* a rock star?

Those who have seen him say the same thing of Bill Clinton. "He's like a rock star!" In other words, the man who, for eight years, was the most powerful man in the world, has attained the same status as someone who bites the heads off of bats.

And it's not just the popularity of the rock star to which we aspire, not only for ourselves but also for our political and religious leaders. There's a transcendent quality that some of our idols possess that attracts us to them. When we see video of early Elvis, Dylan, Hendrix, *Ziggy Stardust*–era Bowie, The Clash, Stevie Ray Vaughn, Cobain, or, yes, even early GNR, they seem to have the gift for a divine sort of communication. The reality, of course, is that this usually turns out to be heroin, but I won't allow that to get in the way of the image.

Since the demise of JFK and MLK, which also marks the emergence of The Beatles and popular music in general as our cultural and philosophical center, how many positive messages have we received from political and religious leaders? Even a speed metal band wouldn't come out with something as dreary as "Axis of Evil." Instead, we take meaning from our rock stars. We find inspiration in a chord change and hope from a simple turn of phrase. I'm not saying it's necessarily a good thing, but it is something.

Not that I or Onyxx or any other member of the Hair Metal community ever achieved such a level of gravity, which is why, save GNR, we don't listen to much Hair Metal these days. But this potential for influence does explain why so many of us try. I may have been a nerd with an absurd fantasy, but so was Brian Wilson. And so was Alice Cooper. And Joey Ramone. And Gene Simmons. And Axl Rose. And Trent Reznor. So that every humiliation and every triumph I experienced in pursuit of my fantasy now seems invaluable to me.

Difficult as it is for me to say, I am no longer a rock star. After all, my best hope for group sex these days is masturbating with two hands. Yet I'm also content in my relationship with my disease. There's nothing I enjoy more than the reaction I get from people when I trot out my old war stories. Usually, they imagine I'm kidding, until I back up my tale of woe and fantasy with anecdotes and photographs too fantastic not to be real. I am a survivor, I tell them, an eyewitness to a glorious age and place, where butt rockers roamed the earth, mingling freely amongst groupies, roadies, and fans.

Perhaps my bigger problem, rather than the disease itself, is that I don't want to get over it. Maybe I'm afraid that I'll confuse my fantasy with my memory, and to disregard one might be to forget the other. Maybe there's a meditative quality to my rock star fantasy now, whether I'm alone with my guitar, in my car, or on an airplane with my headphones on. Maybe a fantasy is the only thing that makes reality bearable, no matter how fantastic the fantasy really is, so long as you don't actually try to live it. But then again, why the hell not?

Maybe the real reason I don't want to get over my fantasy is that I loved every crotch-grabbing, ass-rocking, boob-signing minute of it. And I'll hold on to it as long as I possibly can.

*   *   *

After the break up, I continued to see Tyler and Kyle as our senior year went on, although at an inverse rate to the frequency of their drug use.

Kyle fell deeper and deeper into that world and wound up finishing high school several years after me at a continuation school. The last time I saw Kyle was in the summer of 1992, at the 2nd Annual KROQ Weenie Roast and Sing Along. Despite a line-up that included Beck, Green Day, Pavement, Rollins Band, and The Violent Femmes, Kyle was so out of his mind that we had to leave early.

I haven't heard from him since.

Tyler and I remained close for a couple years after Onyxxx broke up. We never considered starting another band, nor did we ever reminisce about the old one. We gradually lost touch when I went to school and he moved to Kansas, where his father had moved a couple years before. I have no idea where he is today.

Throughout our senior year of high school, Sonny and I rekindled our friendship. He did go on to study at Berkeley, and then on to Yale for a master's in public health, and finally on to Michigan State for his M.D. Today, he's a cardiology fellow somewhere in the Southwest, but he won't allow me to say where. I served as best man in his wedding, and he remains one of my closest friends. We still get together and jam whenever possible.

*   *   *

I never saw Barbi again. Oddly, as I was writing this book, Sonny received an e-mail from her oldest daughter, informing him that Barbi had passed away in Hawaii of heart complications. She was fifty-two years old.

My leather pants died of natural causes in Las Vegas, Nevada.

They were only sixteen.

About the Author

Craig A. Williams attended college at the University of California, Irvine, and received a master's in professional writing at the University of Southern California. He writes for various film and television studios from his home in Santa Monica, California, where he lives with five guitars, two ukuleles, and a mandolin.